THE

SATANIC POPE

ENLIGHTENMENT

(Brief) MASONIC PHILOSOPHY

(1220)

Masonic Satanic Pope; King: Mr.Jaheem R.Hilts
Of The Satanic Kingdom

December 31st, 1986

authorHOUSE

AuthorHouse™
1663 Liberty Drive
Bloomington, IN 47403
www.authorhouse.com
Phone: 1 (800) 839-8640

Published by AuthorHouse 05/15/2020

ISBN: 978-1-7283-6238-0 (sc)
ISBN: 978-1-7283-6237-3 (e)

Library of Congress Control Number: 2020909083

Print information available on the last page.

TABLE OF CONTENT

I decided not to write the last two chapters to this book. The original intent was 13 chapters.........

BOOK TRANSLATED INTO - (Hebrew, Arabic, Chinese, Greek, German, Filipino, French, Dutch, Hindi, Japanese, Irish, Italian, Portuguese, Swedish, Thai, Russian, and Korean)

Satan is not your enemy; man is his own enemy going against his understanding, for his ignorance.
May 8th, 2020 King: Jaheem R.Hilts

Satan brings pieces of lost puzzles together.
May 8th, 2020 King: Jaheem R.Hilts

The Ancient lost knowledge can be found through Satan.
May 8th, 2020 King: Jaheem R.Hilts

Dedications

Aleister Crowley

Anton Lavey

Ozzy Osbourne

Alice Cooper

Marilyn Manson

Gasper Rodriguez

Jayquan Comer

Jaheem R. Hilts

Declaration of Sovereignty Satanic Empire Order

Satanic Sovereignty Order Operator: Mr.Jaheem R.Hilts
The Satanic Pope: Jaheem Rashon Marcus Anthony Hilts

This is documentation of the true existence of a Sovereignty Order, under religious practices. This Order is claiming Ancient practices that should not be interfered with by any Government Laws. We believe in The Creator and we believe in The Laws of The Universe. We believe we have The Rights to function under abilities, in all Satanic practices private or public. Our purpose and cause is to enlighten those we choose; we don't operate by force. We exercise love, peace and harmony in the evolution of humanity. We believe when God casted Satan down to Earth, it formed a Government of intellectual Spiritual Beings that would form a Government for intellectual Humans to follow. This Declaration is only for the chosen, only those initiated.

SOVEREIGN AUTHORITY
Jaheem Rashon Marcus Anthony Hilts
December 31st, 1986
(1220) SECRET SOCIETY

The most knowledgeable will know that Satan has been around longer than mankind. The misunderstanding from the individual comprehension of a person eliminates indulgence into higher acknowledgement. The spirit can only see in darkness, one must be taught the forbidden truth to excel in a travel necessary in all eyes especially the 3rd eye. Satan has revealed secrets of Heaven and Earth to those most trustworthy to him; his cause to make a statement. To believe in the help of Satan, it's partially accepting that even Satan is a part of the whole creation. Why will one look down on what they do not understand? Making excuses for their actions. Satan has a role in things taking place on Earth; some are enjoyable, some as a lesson. Give thanks to Satan for making you stronger, don't give up on yourself. (1220)

Chapter (1): Satan is Ancient

From the beginning of time long before consciousness was even an option, Satan existed. The universe was just full of spirits; other things that were only capable in the unseen world. Intelligence would not even be understood on a human level because humans did not exist, except in a future plan. The activities in these spiritual realms have never been capable of documentation. Satan was before the creativity and structural development of architectural designs by past generations of mankind. Satan is ancient because we can't calculate his time in existence, when he was born or formed. We shall know those in biblical times joined Satan for wisdom and the ability to see further than others. Satan is no fool we all have choices Satan's choice was magnificent in his eyes. Right and wrong are merely by ones perception, sinning has brought happiness to countless amounts of people daily, longer than recognized. Satan doesn't have to think for you, you are a part of the beginning, no matter how much time goes by.

Chapter (2): How to help Satan

You have to realize you helping Satan it's helping you. Satan will want you to have all the pleasures and desires you want for yourself. By helping Satan you will make good of all sins in the world. You help Satan by helping others; people come together and enjoy time with each other in Satan ways, while sin is beautiful, you must spread its beauty. Helping Satan should not be considered a weakness, even though people will frown upon the work. You can help Satan by not being foolish leading by example, creating more peace than those professing to be Godly. You can help Satan by being loyal and trustworthy to The Satan Army. There is a battle between good and evil and Satan doesn't just want to be known for evil; destruction.

4

Chapter (3): Converting to Satan

I wouldn't advise someone to try and understand Satan by themselves. It would be greater to be introduced to The Dark Forces. One can lose hope trying to reach out to Satan without initiation. The ability to convert is like all else, you have to have faith. Faith in Satan may not be easy for everybody because of the negative gossip, recordings of false interpretations. Mind, body and soul have to be in it to receive completion; nothing is whole missing something important. Converting to Satan is sensitive because it's secretive the initial process at least, it's highly beneficial for those destined to convert from their past confusions. I could reference other books to broaden the understanding of this topic. I choose not to because they won't support you converting. Satan represents forbidden knowledge or secret knowledge. Converting to Satan you have to begin developing, after carrying the seeds. They will grow even if you resist yourself. Converting to Satan it's a new beginning, a life with no regrets, if you love knowledge and wisdom.

Chapter (4): Relationships & Satan

True love is easily found in two people wanting to be together, based on trust. It's not anything made off an unconscious decision both will have to want the same thing. The forbidden knowledge that is passed down to the initiate is sufficient in handling a relationship situation. There is a connection that can't be described the world is visualized as more pleasant. There is no uncertainty that can penetrate, nothing unknown that can break you a part, referring to (Dark Forces Energy). Satan is great in keeping his people in awesome relationships, both travelling the path of Satan. Satan can also be noted in making good relationships, when one of his followers is, in a relationship with someone of a different faith. As stated before Satan is ancient so there is no theory that Satan knows about love. There is no question that those on The Satan path will have love with each other, this of course is if they want it. A relationship founded with initiation, is a blessed wild fire contained in a safe place. Emotions influence free will vice versa no task for the weak.

Chapter (5): Wise poetry of Satan

If only you were not misunderstood, how bright will the glow from the sky be? As the formulation of water in the sight of my naked eye leads my mind to ancient times, you appear in glory. The world is a reflection, of your existence. The thoughts are filled with unremarkable pleasures. I see your beauty, I want your company, and I know not to be naive. Through the clouds, if they can hold me standing on them. I will travel the distance; I will anchor occupying nothing except infinite.

1220 (Poetry)

Chapter (6): Community of Satan

Through the ages there have been communities that were driven by Satan. Just because a person chooses to follow the forbidden knowledge and wisdom of Satan doesn't make them less than anyone else sharing planet earth. A community of Satan is a community that deals with rituals. They deal with foreseeing things before they happen and being well prepared. It would be an honor to even be accepted into the activities of such a community, while others may see it different. Look how old the earth is and the different energies; influences most people take in just walking outside or opening a window in the house. When dealing with the wisdom and knowledge one can get from Satan, you will find a lot of happiness, self satisfaction, which even in a basic form is good because learning never stops. The community of Satan should never be discarded because they offer to apply intelligence where it needs to be. Comprehending intelligence is common for even one member of The Satan Path.
(1220)

Chapter (7): How to control your thoughts can Satan help you?

It is important to know that we all have a head full of thoughts and more appear in times of different emotions. For the people that live off The Satan Path, they are familiar with this daily occurrence inside the mind. They have studied themselves to the point they can pick their thoughts like using their hands, instead of the choice of action. Satan plays a major role in this ability because it's encouraged at some point when joining The Satan people. This chapter is touching on awareness of a specific area of topic there is no desire to be to descriptive. One must seek to master themselves in all aspects especially dealing with the mind. Guidance would be better than trying to simply understand something not understandable. Satan wants his people not to be victims of not having self control or thought control.

Chapter (8): The letter from The Satanic Pope (Pope-Jaheem R.Hilts)

The Darkside has been exquisite in the development of intelligence, since its ancient formulation. The Satanic way has been discriminated on because of the misunderstanding of Satan. People rather praise unhealthy acts upon humanity accepting wrong from certain peers or relatives and frown upon someone else's religious belief. For the future of The Satanic all Satanic should show the difference to decrease the ignorance of perception of The Satanic culture. The future of The Satanic shall flourish in happiness in all its affairs. Remind yourself outsiders don't matter if you're doing right, even in private. The growth of The Satanic shall be massive and carefully applied so people can see the truth instead of false dogma. Don't allow peoples ignorance or judgment to make you question reality when it came from their daily illusions/delusion.

Satanic Pope

(1220) *Jaheem R.Hilts*

May 9th, 2020 11:28pm (MST)

Chapter (9): Brief about the unseen world

Once upon a time, in a world only dealing with spirits, there was a constant activity in using supernatural abilities in the unseen world. Everything was happening spirits were giving birth to spirits; spirits went through the process of dying even though they couldn't die. God reigned supreme and everything was illuminated by the royal spirit, The Creator of all in existence. The light from The Throne was the light of the world. Satan was knowledgeable more than all in the spiritual world. He was a master and he spent time pondering the things in existence. The thought crossed God's mind for another part of his creation. Satan was full of joy, he began to play music that pleased God, The Angels even sang. Then God started manifesting things in existence. Satan thought it was an expansion for the unseen world. Satan seen God's glory and beauty, he was tempted to speak when he seen God forming man, then he waited……..

(To be continued)

Biblical Scholar
1220-*Jaheem R. Hilts*

Chapter (10): Satan should be understood and not shunned

If we look at all biblical history mankind has made his own decisions from survival to ability. They say "Lucifer was casted out of Heaven" they say "Adam and Eve were casted from The Garden of Eden". There is no one to blame at the end of the day. Satan shouldn't be shunned especially when one has knowledge of Satan, even if one doesn't. The reason I say this is because everyone has a freewill choice. What good would it be to shun someone and you have the choice to make a decision nobody can make for you. We in The Satanic embrace Satan because he is filled with wisdom that man has no ability to have. We have the slightest insight on the full unseen world. Satan is a different form of creation; those initiated can understand the broadness of how to communicate and understand what they are dealing with. Satan should be understood and not shunned. (1220)

Chapter (11): The entrance is important

It is important to know that the entrance into The Satanic is sensitive, very delicate. It should be a matter taken very seriously and not allowed to be abused. It is a world inside a world, knowledge should not be wasted. Most people will not seek the truth and curiosity is common. The importance is beyond comprehension of the uninitiated. Those with knowledge may want to further spiritual growth; practice the culture of The Satanic unity. How one comes forward with the ability to grow is important, the love for The Satanic must be strong in one practicing initiations on others or failure is possible. As light shines in darkness and darkness shines in light, it will all be. Never seek to make someone else's mind up surrender/submission is for all students.

תורגם לעברית

Hebrew

האדם הבקיא ביותר ידע שהשטן היה בסביבה
יותר זמן מאשר האנושות. אי ההבנה מההבנה
האינדיבידואלית של האדם מבטלת את הפינוק להכרה
הרוח יכולה רק לראות בחשכה, יש ללמד. גבוהה יותר
את האמת האסורה להצטיין בנסיעה הנחוצה בכל
השטן חשף את . העיניים במיוחד בעין השלישית
הסודות של שמים וארץ לאלה האמינים לו ביותר; את.
המטרה שלו להצהיר הצהרה להאמין בעזרתו של
השטן, זה מקבל חלקית שאפילו השטן הוא חלק
למה שמישהו יראה למטה? מה הם לא .מהיצירה כולה
מבינים . מתרץ תירוצים למעשיהם לשטן יש תפקיד
בדברים שמתרחשים בכדור הארץ; חלקם מהנים,
הודה לשטן על שעשה אותך חזק יותר, .חלקם כשיעור
(אל תוותר על עצמך. (1220

15

פרק (1): השטן עתיק

מאז תחילת הזמן הרבה לפני התודעה היתה אפילו אופציה, השטן היה קיים. היקום היה פשוט מלא ברוחות; דברים אחרים שהיו מסוגלים רק בעולם האינטליגנציה לא היתה מובנת אפילו. הבלתי נראה ברמה האנושית משום שבני האדם לא היו קיימים, למעט בתוכנית עתידית. הפעילות במחוזות הרוחניים השטן היה. הללו מעולם לא היתה מסוגלת לתיעוד לפני היצירתיות וההתפתחות הקונסטרוקטיבית של עיצובים אדריכליים בדורות האחרונים של האנושות. השטן הוא עתיק משום שאיננו יכולים לחשב את זמנו אנחנו נדע את אלה. בקיומו, כאשר נולד או נוצר שבתקופת המקרא הצטרפו לשטן לחוכמה וליכולת לראות יותר מהאחרים. השטן הוא לא טיפש, לכולנו יש את האפשרויות. שהבחירה של השטן היתה הנכונות והעוול הן רק בתפיסה הזאת, מרהיבה בעיניו חטא הבא אושר לאינספור כמויות של אנשים מדי יום, יותר מאשר מוכר. השטן לא צריך לחשוב עליך, אתה חלק מההתחלה, לא משנה כמה זמן עובר.

פרק (2): כיצד לעזור לשטן

אתה חייב להבין שאתה עוזר. לשטן שזה עוזר לך השטן ירצה שיהיו לך את כל ההנאות והתשוקות שאתה רוצה בעצמך. על ידי עזרה לשטן, אתה תהיה אתה עוזר לשטן על ידי. טוב מכל החטאים בעולם עזרה לאחרים; אנשים לבוא יחד וליהנות זמן אחד עם השני בדרכים השטן, בעוד החטא הוא יפה, אתה חייב להפיץ את יופיו. לעזור לשטן לא להיחשב לחולשה, אתה יכול. למרות שאנשים מפנים את העבודה בזעף לעזור לשטן בכך שהוא לא יהיה טיפש מוביל בדוגמה, ליצור שלום יותר מאשר אלה שמרים להיות שועל. אתה יכול לעזור לשטן בכך שתהיה נאמן ואמין לצבא השטן. יש קרב בין טוב לרע והשטן לא רק רוצה להיות ידוע לרעה; הרס.

17

פרק (3): המרה לשטן

לא הייתי מייעץ למישהו לנסות. להבין את השטן
בעצמו יהיה גדול יותר להיות מוצג לכוחות האופל. אדם יכול
לאבד תקווה מנסה להגיע אל השטן ללא חניכה. היכולת להמיר
היא כמו כל דבר אחר, אתה חייב להאמין. אמונה בשטן לא יכולה
להיות קלה לכולם בגלל הרכילות השלילית, הקלטות של
הנפש, הגוף והנפש צריכים להיות בו כדי לקבל. פרשנויות שווא
השלמה; . שום דבר לא חסר משהו חשוב המרה לשטן רגישה
משום שהיא מחשאית את התהליך הראשוני לפחות, היא מועילה
מאוד לאלה המיועדים להמיר מלבולים שלהם בעבר. אני יכול
להפנות לספרים אחרים כדי להרחיב את ההבנה של נושא זה.
השטן מייצג אני בוחר שלא משום שהם. לא יתמכו בך בהמרה
ידע אסור או ידע סודי. המרה לשטן אתה צריך להתחיל לפתח,
לאחר נשיאת הזרעים. . הם יגדלו גם אם תתנגד המרה לשטן זו
התחלה חדשה, חיים ללא חרטות, אם אתה אוהב ידע ותבונה.

18

פרק (4): מערכות יחסים & השטן

אהבה אמיתית מתגלה בקלות אצל שני אנשים שרוצים להיות יחד, בהתבסס על אמון.. שניהם צריכים לרצות את אותו הדבר הידע האסור שהועבר ליוזמה מספיק בטיפול במצב מערכת יש חיבור שאי אפשר לתאר את העולם הוא מדמיין יותר. יחסים נעים. אין חוסר ודאות שיכול לחדור, שום דבר לא ידוע שיכול השטן גדול. (לשבור לך חלק, מתייחס (אנרגיה כוחות אפלים בשמירה על אנשיו במערכות יחסים מדהימות, שניהם מטיילים בדרך של השטן. ניתן לציין את השטן גם בעשיית מערכות יחסים טובות, כאשר אחד מחסידיו הוא, במערכת יחסים עם אדם בעל אמונה שונה. כאמור לפני השטן הוא עתיק, כך שאין שום אין ספק כי אלה על השביל. תאוריה שהשטן יודע על אהבה השטן יהיה לאהוב אחד את השני, זה כמובן אם הם רוצים את זה. מערכת יחסים שהוקמה עם חניכה, היא אש פראית מבורכת הכלולה במקום בטוח. השפעה על רגשות חופשית. לא תהיה משימה לחלשים

19

פרק (5): שירה נבונה של השטן

אם רק לא היית מובנת? כמה זוהר יהיה הלהט   ,
מהשמים כניסוח המים במראה עיניי העירומה מוביל את מוחי
לזמנים קדומים, אתה מופיע בתהילה. . העולם הוא השתקפות
של קיומך המחשבות מלאות. בתענוגות לא מראויים אני רואה
את יופייך, אני רוצה את. החברה שלך, ואני יודע שלא להיות
נאיבי דרך העננים, אם הם יכולים. להחזיק אותי עומד עליהם
אני מטייל במרחק; אני עוגן כובש כולם. מלבד אינסוף

1220 (שירה)

20

פרק (6): קהילת השטן

במשך הדורות היו קהילות שהיו מונעים על ידי השטן.
רק בגלל שאדם בוחר ללכת בעקבות הידע והחוכמה האסורים
של השטן, לא הופך אותם לפחות מכל אחר שמשתתף את
כדור הארץ. קהילה של שטן היא קהילה העוסקת בטקסים. הם
מתמודדים עם דברים מראש לפני שהם מתרחשים ומוכנים
זה יהיה כבוד אפילו להתקבל לפעילות של קהילה כזו, .היטב
בעוד שאחרים עשויים לראות אותו שונה. תראו בן כמה האדמה
והאנרגיות השונות; משפיע על רוב האנשים לקחת רק הליכה
בחוץ או לפתוח חלון בבית. כאשר ההתמודדות עם החוכמה
והידע ניתן לקבל מן השטן, תוכלו למצוא הרבה אושר, סיפוק
עצמי, אשר אפילו בצורה בסיסית הוא טוב כי למידה אף פעם לא
הקהילה של השטן לא צריכה להיות מושלך משום שהם. מפסיק
מציעים ליישם מודיעין היכן שהוא צריך להיות. ההבנה הינה
מקובלת אפילו על חבר אחד בנתיב השטן.

(1220)

21

פרק (7): כיצד לשלוט במחשבותיך האם השטן יכול לעזור לך?

חשוב לדעת שכולנו מלאים במחשבות ומופיעים בזמנים של רגשות שונים. עבור האנשים החיים את דרך השטן, הם מכירים את ההתרחשות היומית הזאת בתוך המוח. הם חקרו את עצמם עד כדי כך שהם יכולים לבחור את המחשבות שלהם השטן משחק. כמו להשתמש בידיהם, במקום בבחירת הפעולה תפקיד מרכזי ביכולת זו משום שהוא מעודד בשלב כלשהו בעת הצטרפות לבני השטן. פרק זה נוגע במודעות לתחום מסוים של נושא, אין רצון להיות תיאורי. על האדם לנסות לשלוט בעצמם הדרכה תהיה טובה יותר. בכל ההיבטים העוסקים במחשבה מלנסות פשוט להבין משהו שאינו מובן. השטן רוצה שאנשיו לא יהיו קורבנות של חוסר שליטה עצמית או מחשבה.

22

פרק (8): המכתב מהאפיפיור השטני

הצד האפל היה מעולה בפיתוח של אינטליגנציה, מאז
ניסוח העתיקה שלה. הדרך השטנית הופלה בגלל אי ההבנה של
השטן. אנשים מעדיפים לשבח מעשים לא בריאים על האנושות
המקבל עוול מעמיתים או קרובי משפחה מסוימים וזועף על
האמונה הדתית של מישהו אחר. לעתיד של השטני כל שטני
צריך להראות את ההבדל כדי להקטין את הבורות של תפיסת
עתידה של השטני ישגשג באושר בכל ענייניה. ..התרבות השטנית
להזכיר לעצמכם זרים לא משנה אם אתה עושה נכון, אפילו
בפרטיות. התפתחותם של השטני תהיה מסיבית ומיושמת
בקפידה כך שאנשים יוכלו לראות את האמת במקום את הדוגמה
השקרית. אל תאפשר לאנשים בורות או שיקול דעת לגרום לך
לפקפק במציאות כשזה בא מאשליות/אשליה היומית שלהם.

Satanic Pope
(1220) *Jaheem R.Hilts*
May 9th, 2020 11:28pm (MST)

23

פרק (9): קיצור על העולם הבלתי נראה

פעם, בעולם שהתמודזו רק עם רוחות, הייתה פעילות מתמדת בשימוש ביכולות על-טבעיות בעולם הבלתי נראה. כל מה שקורה במצב רוח הוליד רוחות; רוחות עברו את תהליך המוות למרות שהם לא יכלו למות. אלוהים העליון והכל היה האור . . מואר על ידי הרוח המלכותית, הבורא של כל הקיום מהכס היה אור העולם השטן היה בעל ידע רב יותר מכל העולם הרוחני. הוא היה מאסטר והוא השקיע זמן בלהרהר בדברים הקיימים. המחשבה הצתה את מוחו של אלוהים לחלק אחר של יצירתו. השטן היה מלא שמחה, הוא התחיל לנגן מוזיקה ברצון ואז אלוהים התחיל. לעשות. אלוהים, המלאכים אפילו שרו דברים בקיום השטן חשב שזו התרחבות. של העולם הבלתי נראה השטן ראה את התהילה והיופי של אלוהים, הוא התפתה לדבר כאשר הוא ראה את האדם יוצר האלוהים, ואז חיכה.......

(כדי להמשיך)

Biblical Scholar
1220-*Jaheem R. Hilts*

24

פרק (10): יש להבין את השטן ולא להתרחקו

אם נסתכל על כל ההיסטוריה המקראית המין האנושי קיבל את החלטותיו מהישרדות ליכולת. אומרים "לוציפר הוציא מהשמיים" הם אומרים "אדם וחוה היו מחוץ לגן עדן".‏. אין מי שאשם בסוף היום השטן לא צריך להיות מנמנע במיוחד כאשר לאדם יש ידע על השטן, גם אם לא. הסיבה שאני אומר זאת היא. שלכולם יש בחירה חופשית מה טוב יהיה לשון מישהו ויש לך את הבחירה לקבל החלטה שאף אחד לא יכול לעשות בשבילך. בגלל שהוא מלא בחוכמה. שלאדם אין יכולת לקבל יש לנו שמץ של תובנה. על העולם המלא והבלתי נראה השטן הוא צורה שונה של יצירה; אלה שיזם יכול להבין את הרחבה של איך לתקשר ולהבין עם מה הם מתמודדים. יש להבין את השטן ולא להתרחקו. (1220)

25

פרק (11): הכניסה חשובה

חשוב לדעת שהכניסה לתוך השטני רגישה, מאוד
עדינה. זה צריך להיות עניין שנלקח מאוד ברצינות ולא מורשה
להיות מנוצל. זה עולם בתוך עולם, הידע לא צריך להיות
מבוזבז. רוב האנשים לא יחפשו את האמת והסקרנות נפוצה.
אלה עם ידע. החשיבות היא מעבר להבנה של הבלתי מפותח
עשוי לרצות צמיחה רוחנית נוספת; תרגל את התרבות של
האחדות השטנית. איך מישהו מתקדם עם היכולת לגדול הוא
חשוב, האהבה של השטני חייב להיות חזק באימון אחד על
אחרים או כישלון אפשרי. כאשר אור זורח בחשכה וחשכה
זורחת באור, הכל יהיה. לעולם אל תבקש לגרום למוחו של
מישהו אחר להיכנע/להגשה הוא לכל התלמידים.

26

ترجمت إلى العربية
Arabic

الأكثر دراية سوف نعرف أن الشيطان كان في جميع أنحاء أطول من البشرية. سوء الفهم من الفهم الفردي للشخص يلغي التساهل إلى اعتراف أعلى. الروح يمكن أن نرى فقط في الظلام، يجب أن يعلم المرء الحقيقة المحرمة للتفوق في السفر اللازمة في جميع العيون وخاصة العين

3. لقد كشف الشيطان أسرار السماء والأرض لأولئك الأكثر جدارة بالثقة بالنسبة له. قضيته للادلاء ببيان للإيمان بمساعدة الشيطان، فإنه يقبل جزئيا أنه حتى الشيطان هو جزء من الخليقة بأكملها. لماذا ينظر المرء إلى ما لا يفهمه؟ تقديم الأعذار لأفعالهم. الشيطان له دور في الأشياء التي تحدث على الأرض. بعضها ممتع، وبعضها كدرس. اشكر الشيطان على اجتماك أقوى، لا تتخلى عن نفسك. (1220)

الفصل (1): الشيطان قديم

منذ بداية الزمن قبل فترة طويلة من أن يكون الوعي خيارًا، كان الشيطان موجودًا. كان الكون مليئاً بالأرواح. أشياء أخرى كانت قادرة فقط في العالم الغيب. الذكاء لن يفهم حتى على المستوى البشري لأن البشر لم يكونوا موجودين، إلا في خطة مستقبلية. لم تكن الأنشطة في هذه العوالم الروحية قادرة على التوثيق. كان الشيطان قبل الإبداع والتطوير الهيكلي للتصاميم المعمارية من قبل الأجيال الماضية من البشرية. الشيطان قديم لأننا لا نستطيع حساب وقته في الوجود، عندما ولد أو تشكل. سنعرف أن أولئك الذين انضموا في زمن الكتاب المقدس إلى الشيطان للحكمة والقدرة على الرؤية أبعد من الشيطان ليس أحمق لدينا جميعا خيارات كان. الآخرين اختيار الشيطان رائعة في عينيه. الصواب والخطأ هي مجرد واحد من التصور، والخطيئة جلبت السعادة لكميات لا تحصى من الناس يوميا، أطول مما هو معترف بها. ليس على الشيطان أن يفكر من أجلك، أنت جزء من البداية، مهما مر الوقت.

الفصل (2): كيفية مساعدة الشيطان

عليك أن تدرك أنك تساعد الشيطان انها تساعدك.
الشيطان سوف تريد لك أن يكون كل الملذات والرغبات
التي تريدها لنفسك. من خلال مساعدة الشيطان سوف
تجعل جيدة من جميع الخطايا في العالم. أنت تساعد
الشيطان من خلال مساعدة الآخرين. الناس معا والتمتع
الوقت مع بعضها البعض بطرق الشيطان، في حين أن
مساعدة الشيطان لا. الخطيئة جميلة، يجب أن تنتشر جمالها
ينبغي أن تعتبر نقطة ضعف، على الرغم من أن الناس
سوف يعبس ونعابس على العمل. يمكنك مساعدة الشيطان
من خلال عدم الحماقة الرائدة بالقدوة، وخلق المزيد من
يمكنك مساعدة. السلام من أولئك الذين يعلنون أن يكون الله
الشيطان من خلال الولاء والثقة لجيش الشيطان. هناك
معركة بين الخير والشر والشيطان لا يريد فقط أن يكون
معروفا بالشر. تدمير

الفصل (3): التحول إلى الشيطان

لا أنصح أحداً أن يحاول فهم الشيطان بنفسه سيكون من الأعظم أن يتم تعريفي لقوى الظلام يمكن للمرء أن يفقد الأمل في محاولة للوصول إلى الشيطان دون البدء. القدرة على تحويل مثل كل شيء آخر، عليك أن يكون الإيمان. قد لا يكون الإيمان بالشيطان سهلاً على الجميع بسبب القيل والقال السلبي، تسجيلات التفسيرات العقل والجسد والروح يجب أن يكون في ذلك للحصول على. الخاطئة الانتهاء؛ لا شيء كله في عداد المفقودين شيء مهم. التحول إلى الشيطان أمر حساس لأنه سري العملية الأولية على الأقل ، إنه مفيد للغاية لأولئك الذين تم مقدر لهم التحول من إرباكاتهم السابقة. ويمكنني أن أشير إلى كتب أخرى لتوسيع نطاق فهم هذا الموضوع. الشيطان يمثل المعرفة. اخترت عدم لأنها لن تدعم تحويل لك المحرمة أو المعرفة السرية. تحويل إلى الشيطان لديك لبدء النامية، بعد حمل البذور. سوف تنمو حتى لو قاومت نفسك. التحول إلى الشيطان انها بداية جديدة، حياة مع أي ندم، إذا كنت تحب المعرفة والحكمة.

الفصل (4): العلاقات والشيطان

الحب الحقيقي يمكن العثور عليه بسهولة في شخصين
يريدان أن يكونا معاً، بناءً على الثقة. انها ليست أي شيء اتخذ من
قرار اللاوعي على حد سواء سوف تضطر إلى تريد نفس الشيء.
المعرفة المحرمة التي يتم تمريرها إلى المبادرة كافية في التعامل مع
حالة العلاقة. هناك اتصال لا يمكن وصفه العالم هو تصور أكثر
متعة. ليس هناك عدم يقين التي يمكن أن تخترق، لا شيء غير
معروف التي يمكن أن كسر لك جزء، في اشارة الى (طاقة قوى
الشيطان هو عظيم في الحفاظ على شعبه في علاقات رهيبة، .(الظلام
وكلاهما السفر على طريق الشيطان. يمكن أيضًا ملاحظة الشيطان
في إقامة علاقات جيدة ، عندما يكون أحد أتباعه ، في علاقة مع
شخص من إيمان مختلف. كما ذكر قبل الشيطان قديم لذلك لا توجد
نظرية أن الشيطان يعرف عن الحب. ليس هناك شك في أن أولئك
الذين على طريق الشيطان سيكون لهم الحب مع بعضهم البعض،
وهذا بالطبع إذا كانوا يريدون ذلك. علاقة تأسست مع بدء، هو النار
العواطف تؤثر على الإرادة. البرية المباركة الواردة في مكان آمن
الحرة العكس بالعكس أي مهمة للضعفاء.

الفصل (5): الشعر الحكيم للشيطان

لو لم يساء فهمك، فكم سيكون التوهج من السماء مشرقاً؟
كما صياغة الماء في مرأى من عيني المجردة يقود ذهني إلى العصور القديمة، تظهر في المجد. العالم هو انعكاس لوجودك الأفكار مليئة بالملذات غير الملحوظة. أرى جمالك، أريد صحبتك، وأعلم أن لا أكون ساذجاً. من خلال الغيوم، إذا استطاعوا أن يحملوني واقفاً عليهم. سأقطع المسافة. سأستور احتلال لا شيء إلا اللانهائي.

1220 (شعر)

33

الفصل (6): مجتمع الشيطان

على مر العصور كانت هناك مجتمعات كان يقودها الشيطان. فقط لأن الشخص يختار اتباع المعرفة المحرمة والحكمة من الشيطان لا يجعلها أقل من أي شخص آخر تقاسم كوكب الأرض. مجتمع الشيطان هو مجتمع يتعامل مع الطقوس. وهي تتعامل مع التنبؤ بالأمور قبل حدوثها والاستعداد بشكل جيد. سيكون شرفاً لي أن يتم قبولي في أنشطة مثل هذا المجتمع، في حين أن الآخرين قد يرون انظروا كم عمر الأرض والطاقات المختلفة. يؤثر على. الأمر مختلفاً معظم الناس في مجرد المشي خارج أو فتح نافذة في المنزل. عند التعامل مع الحكمة والمعرفة يمكن للمرء أن يحصل من الشيطان، وسوف تجد الكثير من السعادة، والرضا عن النفس، والتي حتى في شكل أساسي هو جيد لأن التعلم لا يتوقف أبدا. لا ينبغي أبداً نبذ مجتمع الشيطان لأنهم يعرضون تطبيق الذكاء حيث يجب أن يكون. فهم الذكاء أمر شائع حتى لعضو واحد من مسار الشيطان.

(1220)

الفصل (7): كيف يمكن السيطرة على أفكارك الشيطان مساعدتك؟

من المهم أن نعرف أن لدينا جميعا رئيس كامل من الأفكار وأكثر تظهر في أوقات المشاعر المختلفة. بالنسبة للأشخاص الذين يعيشون على طريق الشيطان، فهم على دراية بهذا الحدث اليومي داخل العقل. لقد درسوا أنفسهم لدرجة أنهم يستطيعون اختيار أفكارهم مثل استخدام أيديهم ، بدلاً من اختيار العمل. الشيطان يلعب دورا رئيسيا في هذه القدرة لأنه يشجع في مرحلة ما عند الانضمام إلى شعب الشيطان. هذا الفصل هو لمس على الوعي من مجال معين من يجب على المرء أن. الموضوع ليس هناك رغبة في أن يكون وصفيا يسعى إلى السيطرة على أنفسهم في جميع الجوانب وخاصة التعامل مع العقل. التوجيه سيكون أفضل من محاولة فهم شيء ببساطة لا يمكن فهمه. الشيطان يريد شعبه أن لا يكون ضحية لعدم وجود السيطرة على النفس أو السيطرة على الفكر.

(الفصل (8): رسالة البابا الشيطاني (البابا جهيم ر. هيلتس

كان الجانب المظلم رائعًا في تطوير الذكاء ، منذ صياغته القديمة. الطريقة الشيطانية تم التمييز عليها بسبب سوء فهم الشيطان. الناس بدلا من الثناء على الأعمال غير الصحية على الإنسانية قبول الخطأ من بعض الأقران أو الأقارب وعبس على المعتقد الديني لشخص آخر. من أجل مستقبل الشيطان كل شيطاني ينبغي أن تظهر مستقبل الشيطان. الفرق للحد من الجهل من تصور الثقافة الشيطانية سيزدهر في السعادة في جميع شؤونه. تذكر نفسك الغرباء لا يهم إذا كنت تفعل الحق، حتى في القطاع الخاص. نمو الشيطان يجب أن تكون ضخمة وتطبيقها بعناية حتى يتمكن الناس من رؤية الحقيقة بدلا من العقيدة كاذبة. لا تسمح للشعوب الجهل أو الحكم لجعل لكم السؤال الواقع عندما جاء من أوهامهم اليومية / الوهم.

Satanic Pope

(1220) *Jaheem R. Hilts*

May 9th, 2020 11:28pm (MST)

الفصل (9): نبذة عن العالم الغيبي

ذات مرة، في عالم يتعامل فقط مع الأرواح، كان هناك نشاط مستمر في استخدام قدرات خارقة للطبيعة في العالم الغيب. كل شيء كان يحدث الأرواح كانت تلد الأرواح. الأرواح مرت بعملية الموت على الرغم من أنها لا يمكن أن تموت. حكم الله العليا وكان كل شيء مضاءة من قبل الروح الملكية، خالق الجميع في الوجود. الضوء من العرش كان نور العالم. كان الشيطان على دراية أكثر من الجميع في العالم الروحي. كان سيداً وقضى بعض الوقت يتأمل الفكر خطر بعقل الله لجزء آخر من خلقه. كان الأشياء الموجودة الشيطان مليئاً بالفرح، وبدأ يعزف الموسيقى التي أسعدت الله، حتى الملائكة غنوا. ثم بدأ الله يظهر الأشياء في الوجود. الشيطان ظن أنه توسع للعالم الغيب رأى الشيطان مجد الله وجماله، وكان يميل إلى الكلام عندما رأى الله يشكل الإنسان، ثم انتظر.........

(على أن يستمر)

Biblical Scholar

1220-*Jaheem R.Hilts*

الفصل (10): يجب فهم الشيطان وعدم تجنبه

إذا نظرنا إلى كل التاريخ الكتابي البشرية قد اتخذت قراراته الخاصة من البقاء على قيد الحياة إلى القدرة. يقولون "لوسيفر تم طردها من السماء" يقولون "آدم وحواء تم طرحها من جنة عدن". لا يوجد أحد لإلقاء اللوم عليه في نهاية اليوم. لا ينبغي تجنب الشيطان خاصة عندما يكون المرء على علم بالشيطان، حتى لو لم يكن لديه. السبب في قولي هذا هو أن كل شخص لديه خيار الإرادة الحرة. ما فائدة تجنب شخص ما ولديك خيار اتخاذ قرار لا يمكن لأحد أن يتخذ نحن في الشيطان الاحتضان الشيطاني لأنه مليء بالحكمة التي لا لك. يملك الإنسان القدرة على الحصول عليها. لدينا أدنى فكرة عن العالم الغيب الكامل. الشيطان هو شكل مختلف من أشكال الخلق. يمكن لأولئك الذين بدأوا فهم مدى اتساع كيفية التواصل وفهم ما يتعاملون معه. (1220) يجب فهم الشيطان وعدم تجنبه

الفصل (11): المدخل مهم

من المهم أن نعرف أن المدخل إلى الشيطان حساس وحساس جداً. وينبغي أن تؤخذ مسألة على محمل الجد ولا يسمح بإساءة استعمالها. إنه عالم داخل عالم، والمعرفة لا ينبغي أن تضيع. معظم الناس لن يبحثوا عن الحقيقة والفضول شائع. الأهمية لا يمكن فهمها من غير المستهلين. أولئك الذين لديهم المعرفة قد ترغب في كيف يأتي. تعزيز النمو الروحي؛ ممارسة ثقافة الوحدة الشيطانية المرء إلى الأمام مع القدرة على النمو مهم، الحب لالشيطانية يجب أن تكون قوية في واحدة ممارسة البدايات على الآخرين أو الفشل هو ممكن. كما يضيء الضوء في الظلام والظلام يضيء في الضوء، وسوف يكون كل شيء. لا تسعى أبدا لجعل شخص آخر حتى التفكير الاستسلام / تقديم هو لجميع الطلاب.

翻译成中文

Chinese

最有见识的人会知道，萨坦比人类在身边的时间要长。对个人理解的误解消除了对一个人的宽容，从而消除了更高的承认。精神只能在黑暗中看到，必须教导一个人被禁止的真理，才能在所有眼睛，尤其是第三只眼睛的旅行时表现出色。萨坦向那些最值得他信任的人透露了天地的秘密;**他的理由，使一个声明。相信**萨坦的帮助，它部分地接受，甚至萨坦是整个造物的一部分。为什么要看他们不明白的东西呢？为他们的行为找借口。萨坦在地球上发生的事情中起着一定的作用;**有些是令人愉快的，有些是作**为一个教训。感谢萨坦让你更坚强，不要放弃自己。(1220)

第（1）：萨坦是古代的

从意识甚至成为一种选择之前很久开始，萨坦就存在了。宇宙只是充满了精神;**其他的**东西，只有在看不见的世界。智力甚至不会在人类层面上被理解，因为人类并不存在，除非是未来的计划。这些精神领域的活动从未能够记录。萨坦是人类几代人建筑设计的创造力和结构发展之前。萨坦是古老的，因为我们不能计算他的存在时间，当他出生或形成。我们将知道那些在圣经时代加入萨坦的智慧和能力，看到比别人更远。萨坦不是傻瓜，我们都有选择，萨坦的选择在他眼里是宏伟的。对与错只是由一个人感知，罪过每天给无数人带来幸福，比公认的时间长。萨坦不必为你着想，你是开始的开始的一部分，不管时间过得多少。

第（2）：如何帮助萨坦

你必须意识到你帮助萨坦，它帮助你。萨坦会希望你拥有所有你想要的快乐和欲望。通过帮助萨坦，你会使世界上所有的辛斯都好。你帮助别人帮助萨坦;**人**们聚在一起，以萨坦的方式享受彼此的时间，而辛是美丽的，你必须传播它的美丽。**帮助**萨坦不应该被视为一种弱点，即使人们会不赞成这项工作。你可以帮助萨坦，不傻以身作则，创造比那些自称虔诚的人更多的和平。你可以通过忠诚和值得信赖的萨坦军队来帮助萨坦。善与恶之间有一场战斗，而萨坦不仅希望以邪恶著称，破坏。

第（3）：转换为《萨坦》

我不建议别人自己去理解萨坦。引入黑暗势力会更大。一个人可能会失去希望，试图接触萨坦没有启动。转换的能力就像其他一切一样，你必须有信心。对萨坦的信仰可能不容易，因为负面的八卦，虚假的解释录音。心灵、身体和灵魂必须留在其中才能得到完成;**没有什么是整个**错过的东西重要。转换为 Satan **是敏感的**，因为它至少是秘密的初始过程，它对那些注定要从过去的混乱转换是非常有益的。我可以参考其他书籍来扩大对这个话题的理解。我选择不，因为他们不会支持你转换。萨坦代表被禁止的知识或秘密知识。转换到萨坦，你必须开始开发后，携带种子。**即使你抗拒自己，它**们也会增长。转换到萨坦这是一个新的开始，一个没有遗憾的生活，如果你爱知识和智慧。

第（4）：关系与萨坦

真爱很容易在两个人中找到，他们都想在一起，建立在信任的基础上。这不是任何无意识的决定，两人都想要同样的事情。传递给启动者的禁止知识足以处理关系情况。有一种连接是不能形容的，世界被想象为更令人愉快。没有不确定性可以穿透，没有什么未知的，可以打破你的一个部分，指的是（黑暗力量能量）。萨坦是伟大的保持他的人民在真棒关系，都旅行的萨坦之路。当萨坦的追随者之一与不同信仰的人建立关系时，也可**以看到**萨坦建立良好的关系。正如《萨坦》之前所说，萨坦是古代的，所以没有萨坦知道爱情的理论。毫无疑问，在萨坦之路上的人会彼此相爱，这当然是他们想要的话。与启动建立的关系，是一个祝福的野火，包含在一个安全的地方。情绪影响自由，反之亦然，弱者没有任务。

第（5章）：萨坦的睿智诗

要是你没有被误解，天空的光芒会多么明亮？当肉眼眼中的水的配方将我的心引向远古时代时，你显得光彩。世界是你们存在的反映。思想充满了无足轻重的快乐。我看到你的美貌，我想要你的陪伴，我知道不要天真。穿过云层，如果他们能让我站在他们**身上。我会走**远路;**我将**锚占据除了无限。

1220 （诗歌）

第（6）：萨坦社区

古往今来，一些社区一直由萨坦推动。仅仅因为一个人选择遵循萨坦的禁止的知识和智慧，并不能使他们比分享地球的人少。萨坦社区是一个处理仪式的社区。他们处理预见事情之前，他们发生和准备充分。即使被接纳参加这样一个社区的活动，其他人可能会有不同的看法，这将是一种荣誉。看看地球有多古老，不同的能量；影响大多数人采取只是走出去或打开一个窗口的房子。当处理从萨坦得到的智慧和知识时，你会发现很多快乐，自我满足，即使在基本形式是好的，因为学习永远不会停止。不应抛弃萨坦社区，因为它们愿意在需要的地方应用智能。理解智慧对于《萨坦之路》中的一个成员来说也是很常见的。

（1220）

第（7章）：如何控制你的想法，萨坦能帮助你吗？

重要的是要知道，我们都有一个头脑充满了思想，更多的出现在不同情绪的时代。对于生活在《萨坦之路》上的人们来说，他们熟悉了心灵中每天发生的事情。他们已经研究自己，他们可以选择他们的想法，如使用他们的手，而不是选择行动。萨坦在这种能力中起着重要的作用，因为加入萨坦人时，它在某个时候受到鼓励。本章涉及对特定主题领域的认识，无意描述性。**一个人必**须力求从各方面掌握自己，特别是处理思想问题。指导比简单地理解一些不可理解的东西要好。萨坦希望他的人不要成为没有自我控制或思想控制的受害者。

第（8章）：撒旦教皇的信（教皇贾希姆·希尔茨）

　　黑暗边在智力发展方面一直很精致，因为它的古代配方。由于对撒旦的误解，撒旦的方式受到了歧视。人们更赞美人类接受某些同龄人或亲戚错误的不健康行为，并不赞成别人的宗教信仰。对于撒旦的未来，所有撒旦应该表现出差异，以减少对撒旦文化的无知。**撒旦的未来将在其所有事**务中幸福地繁荣起来。提醒自己，外人不管你做得是否正确，即使是私下**里**。**撒旦的成长**应该是大规模和精心应用，以便人们可以看到真相，而不是虚假的教条。不要让人们无知或判断，使你质疑现实，当它来自他们每天的幻想/**幻想**。

Satanic Pope

(1220) *Jaheem R.Hilts*

May 9th, 2020 11:28pm (MST)

第（9）：关于看不见的世界简介

从前，在一个只处理灵魂的世界里，在看不见的世界里，使用超自然能力的活动是不断的。一切都在发生，精神正在产生精神;**精神**经历了死亡的过程，即使他们不能死。上帝统治至高无上，一切都被皇家精神照亮，所有存在的造物主。来自王位的光是世界之光。**在精神世界里**，萨坦比所有人更博学。他是个大师，他花时间思考现存的东西。这一思想在上帝的脑海中浮现，成为他创造的另一部分。萨坦充满了喜悦，他开始演奏音乐，高兴上帝，天使甚至唱。然后上帝开始显现存在的东西。萨坦认为这是对看不见的世界的扩张。萨坦看到了神的荣耀和美丽，当他看到上帝形成人时，他很想说话，然后他等待着……

Biblical Scholar
1220-*Jaheem R.Hilts*

第（10章）：应该理解并避免

如果我们看一下所有圣经历史，人类就做出了从生存到能力自己的决定。他们说"**路西弗被赶出天堂**"，**他**们说"亚当和夏娃是从伊甸园铸造的"。**最后没有人可以**责怪。萨坦不应该回避，尤其是当一个人知道萨坦，即使一个人不知道。我之所以这样说，是因为每个人都有自由意志的选择。回避某人会有什么好，你可以选择做出一个没有人能为你做出的决定。**我**们在撒旦拥抱撒旦，因为他充满了智慧，人类没有能力。我们对这个看不见的世界有丝毫的洞察力。萨坦是一种不同的创造形式;**那些**发起的人可以**理解如何沟通和理解他**们正在处理的事情的广泛性。应该理解，而不是回避。(1220)

第（11）：入口很重要

重要的是要知道，进入撒旦的入口是敏感的，非常微妙的。这件事应该认真对待，不允许被滥用。这是一个世界内部的世界，知识不应该被浪费。大多数人不会寻求真理，好奇心是常见的。重要性是无法理解的。**那些有知**识的人可能想要进一步的精神成长;实践撒旦团结的文化。如何提高成长能力很重要，对撒旦的热爱必须强烈，在练习他人的练习中，否则失败是可能的。当光明在黑暗中闪耀，黑暗在光中闪耀时，一切都将一样。永远不要试图使别人的头脑投降/**服从是所有学生**。

Μεταφρασμένο στα Ελληνικά
Greek

Οι πιο γνώστες θα ξέρουν ότι ο Σατανάς υπάρχει περισσότερο ς καιρός από την ανθρωπότητα. Η παρεξήγηση από την ατομική κατανόηση ενός ατόμου εξαλείφει την επιείκεια σε υψηλότερη αναγνώριση. Το πνεύμα μπορεί να δει μόνο στο σκοτάδι, πρέπει κανείς να διδαχθεί την απαγορευμένη αλήθεια για να υπερέχει σε ένα ταξίδι απαραίτητο σε όλα τα μάτια ειδικά το 3ο μάτι. Ο Σατανάς έχει αποκαλύψει μυστικά του Ουρανού και της Γης σε εκείνους που είναι πιο αξιόπιστοι για αυτόν. την αιτία του να κάνει μια δήλωση. Το να πιστεύεις στη βοήθεια του Σατανά, είναι εν μέρει αποδεκτό ότι ακόμα και ο Σατανάς είναι μέρος ολόκληρης της δημιουργίας. Γιατί κάποιος θα κοιτάξει κάτω σε αυτό που δεν καταλαβαίνουν; Δικαιολογούσε τις πράξεις τους. Ο Σατανάς έχει ένα ρόλο στα πράγματα που λαμβάνουν χώρα στη Γη? μερικά είναι ευχάριστη, μερικά ως μάθημα.

Ευχαρίστησε τον Σατανά που σε έκανε δυνατότερο, μην εγκαταλείπεις τον εαυτό σου. (1220)

Κεφάλαιο (1): Ο Σατανάς είναι Αρχαίος

Από την αρχή του χρόνου πολύ πριν η συνείδηση ήταν ακόμη και μια επιλογή, ο Σατανάς υπήρχε. Το σύμπαν ήταν γεμάτο πνεύματα. άλλα πράγματα που ήταν ικανά μόνο στον αόρατο κόσμο. Νοημοσύνη δεν θα ήταν καν κατανοητή σε ανθρώπινο επίπεδο, επειδή οι άνθρωποι δεν υπήρχαν, εκτός από ένα μελλοντικό σχέδιο. Οι δραστηριότητες σε αυτά τα πνευματικά θέματα δεν ήταν ποτέ ικανές για τεκμηρίωση. Ο Σατανάς ήταν πριν από τη δημιουργικότητα και τη δομική ανάπτυξη αρχιτεκτονικών σχεδίων από τις προηγούμενες γενιές της ανθρωπότητας. Ο Σατανάς είναι αρχαίος επειδή δεν μπορούμε να υπολογίσουμε το χρόνο του στην ύπαρξη, όταν γεννήθηκε ή σχηματίστηκε. Θα γνωρίζουμε εκείνους σε βιβλική εποχή προσχώρησαν Σατανά για τη σοφία και την ικανότητα να δούμε περισσότερο από τους άλλους. Ο Σατανάς δεν είναι ανόητος που όλοι έχουμε επιλογές η επιλογή του Σατανά ήταν υπέροχη στα μάτια του. Το σωστό και το λάθος είναι απλώς από αυτούς αντίληψη, αμαρτία έχει φέρει την ευτυχία σε αμέτρητες ποσότητες ανθρώπων καθημερινά, περισσότερο από ό, τι αναγνωρίζεται. Ο Σατανάς δεν χρειάζεται να σκέφτεται για σένα, είσαι μέρος της αρχής, όσο χρόνο κι αν περάσει.

Κεφάλαιο (2): Πώς να βοηθήσει τον Σατανά

Πρέπει να καταλάβεις ότι βοηθάς τον Σατανά σε βοηθάει. Ο Σατανάς θα θέλει να έχεις όλες τις απολαύσεις και τις επιθυμίες που θέλεις για τον εαυτό σου. Βοηθώντας τον Σατανά θα κάνεις καλό σε όλες τις αμαρτιές του κόσμου. Βοηθάς τον Σατανά βοηθώντας τους άλλους. Οι άνθρωποι ενώνονται και απολαμβάνουν χρόνο μεταξύ τους με τους τρόπους του Σατανά, ενώ η αμαρτία είναι όμορφη, πρέπει να διαδώσετε την ομορφιά της. Η βοήθεια του Σατανά δεν πρέπει να θεωρείται αδυναμία, παρόλο που οι άνθρωποι θα συνοφρυώνονται από το έργο. Μπορείτε να βοηθήσετε τον Σατανά με το να μην είναι ανόητος που οδηγεί με το παράδειγμα, δημιουργώντας περισσότερη ειρήνη από εκείνους που ισχυρίζονται ότι είναι θεϊκοί. Μπορείς να βοηθήσεις τον

Σατανά με το να είσαι πιστός και αξιόπιστος στον Σατανά Στρατό. Υπάρχει μια μάχη μεταξύ καλού και κακού και ο Σατανάς δεν θέλει απλώς να είναι γνωστός για το κακό. Καταστροφή.

Κεφάλαιο (3): Μετατροπή σε Σατανά

Δεν θα συμβούλευα κάποιον να προσπαθήσει να καταλάβει τον Σατανά μόνος του. Θα ήταν μεγαλύτερο να συστηθεί στις Σκοτεινές Δυνάμεις. Κάποιος μπορεί να χάσει την ελπίδα προσπαθώντας να φτάσει στον Σατανά χωρίς μύηση. Η ικανότητα να προσηλυτίσεις είναι όπως όλες οι άλλες, πρέπει να έχεις πίστη. Η πίστη στον Σατανά μπορεί να μην είναι εύκολη για όλους λόγω των αρνητικών κουτσομπολιών, των ηχογραφήσεων ψευδών ερμηνειών. Το μυαλό, το σώμα και η ψυχή πρέπει να είναι σε αυτό για να λάβουν την ολοκλήρωση? τίποτα δεν είναι ολόκληρο λείπει κάτι σημαντικό. Η μετατροπή στον Σατανά είναι ευαίσθητη επειδή είναι μυστικοπαθής η αρχική διαδικασία τουλάχιστον, είναι ιδιαίτερα ευεργετική για εκείνους που προορίζονται να μετατρέψουν από τις προηγούμενες συγχύσεις τους. Θα μπορούσα να αναφερθώ σε άλλα βιβλία για να διευρύνω την κατανόηση αυτού του θέματος. Επιλέγω να μην το κάνω γιατί δεν θα σε υποστηρίξουν να προσηλυτίσεις. Ο Σατανάς αντιπροσωπεύει απαγορευμένη γνώση ή μυστική γνώση. Μετατρέποντας σε Σατανά θα πρέπει να αρχίσει την ανάπτυξη, μετά τη μεταφορά των σπόρων. Θα μεγαλώσουν ακόμα κι αν αντισταθείς στον εαυτό σου. Η μετατροπή στον Σατανά είναι μια νέα αρχή, μια ζωή χωρίς τύψεις, αν αγαπάς τη γνώση και τη σοφία.

Κεφάλαιο (4): Σχέσεις & Σατανάς

Η αληθινή αγάπη βρίσκεται εύκολα σε δύο ανθρώπους που θέλουν να είναι μαζί, με βάση την εμπιστοσύνη. Δεν είναι τίποτα που γίνεται από μια ασυνείδητη απόφαση και οι δύο θα πρέπει να θέλουν το ίδιο πράγμα. Η απαγορευμένη γνώση που διαβιβάζεται στον εκκινητή είναι επαρκής για το χειρισμό μιας κατάστασης σχέσης. Υπάρχει μια σύνδεση που δεν μπορεί να περιγραφεί ο κόσμος απεικονίζεται ως πιο ευχάριστη. Δεν υπάρχει καμία αβεβαιότητα που μπορεί να διεισδύσει, τίποτα άγνωστο που μπορεί να σας σπάσει ένα μέρος, αναφερόμενος στην (Dark Forces Energy). Ο Σατανάς είναι σπουδαίος στο να κρατάει τους ανθρώπους του σε φοβερές σχέσεις, και οι δύο να ταξιδεύουν στο μονοπάτι του Σατανά. Ο Σατανάς μπορεί επίσης να σημειωθεί στο να κάνει καλές σχέσεις, όταν ένας από τους οπαδούς του είναι, σε μια σχέση με κάποιον διαφορετικής πίστης. Όπως αναφέρθηκε πριν ο Σατανάς είναι αρχαίος, οπότε δεν υπάρχει θεωρία ότι ο Σατανάς γνωρίζει για την αγάπη. Δεν υπάρχει αμφιβολία ότι εκείνοι στο μονοπάτι του Σατανά θα έχουν αγάπη μεταξύ τους, αυτό φυσικά είναι αν το θέλουν. Μια σχέση που ιδρύθηκε με την μύηση, είναι μια ευλογημένη άγρια φωτιά που περιέχεται σε ένα ασφαλές μέρος. Τα συναισθήματα επηρεάζουν την ελεύθερη θα αντιστρόφως δεν έργο για τους αδύναμους.

Κεφάλαιο (5): Σοφή ποίηση του Σατανά

Αν δεν παρεξηγήθηκες, πόσο φωτεινή θα είναι η λάμψη από τον ουρανό; Καθώς η διαμόρφωση του νερού στη θέα του γυμνού μου ματιού οδηγεί το μυαλό μου στην αρχαιότητα, εμφανίζεσαι στη δόξα. Ο κόσμος είναι μια αντανάκλαση της ύπαρξής σου. Οι σκέψεις είναι γεμάτες με αξιοσημείωτες απολαύσεις. Βλέπω την ομορφιά σου, θέλω την παρέα σου, και ξέρω ότι δεν είμαι αφελής. Μέσα από τα σύννεφα, αν μπορούν να με κρατήσουν να στέκομαι πάνω τους. Θα διανύω την απόσταση. Θα αγκυροβολήσω καταλαμβάνοντας τίποτα εκτός από άπειρο.

1220 (Ποίηση)

Κεφάλαιο (6): Κοινότητα του Σατανά

Μέσα από τις ηλικίες υπήρξαν κοινότητες που οδηγήθηκαν από τον Σατανά. Ακριβώς επειδή ένα άτομο επιλέγει να ακολουθήσει την απαγορευμένη γνώση και σοφία του Σατανά δεν τους κάνει λιγότερο από οποιονδήποτε άλλο μοιράζονται πλανήτη γη. Μια κοινότητα του Σατανά είναι μια κοινότητα που ασχολείται με τελετουργίες. Ασχολούνται με την επίβλεψη των πραγμάτων πριν συμβούν και να είναι καλά προετοιμασμένοι. Θα ήταν τιμή μου να γίνουν αποδεκτές ακόμη και στις δραστηριότητες μιας τέτοιας κοινότητας, ενώ άλλοι μπορεί να το δουν διαφορετικά. Κοιτάξτε πόσο παλιά είναι η γη και τις διαφορετικές ενέργειες; επιρροές οι περισσότεροι άνθρωποι παίρνουν ακριβώς να περπατήσουν έξω ή να ανοίξουν ένα παράθυρο στο σπίτι. Όταν ασχολείται με τη σοφία και τη γνώση μπορεί κανείς να πάρει από τον Σατανά, θα βρείτε πολλή ευτυχία, αυτοικανοποίηση, η οποία ακόμη και σε μια βασική μορφή είναι καλή, διότι η μάθηση δεν σταματά ποτέ. Η κοινότητα του Σατανά δεν πρέπει ποτέ να απορρίπτεται επειδή προσφέρουν να εφαρμόσουν πληροφορίες εκεί που πρέπει να είναι. Η κατανοώντας νοημοσύνη είναι κοινή ακόμη και για ένα μέλος της διαδρομής του Σατανά.

(1220)

Κεφάλαιο (7): Πώς να ελέγχετε τις σκέψεις σας μπορεί ο Σατανάς να σας βοηθήσει;

Είναι σημαντικό να γνωρίζουμε ότι όλοι έχουμε ένα κεφάλι γεμάτο σκέψεις και περισσότερο εμφανίζονται σε περιόδους διαφορετικών συναισθημάτων. Για τους ανθρώπους που ζουν από το Μονοπάτι του Σατανά, είναι εξοικειωμένοι με αυτό το καθημερινό περιστατικό μέσα στο μυαλό. Έχουν μελετήσει τον εαυτό τους σε σημείο που μπορούν να επιλέξουν τις σκέψεις τους, όπως χρησιμοποιώντας τα χέρια τους, αντί για την επιλογή της δράσης. Ο Σατανάς παίζει σημαντικό ρόλο σε αυτή την ικανότητα, επειδή ενθαρρύνεται κάποια στιγμή όταν ενώνει τον λαό του Σατανά. Το κεφάλαιο αυτό αγγίζει την ευαισθητοποίηση για ένα συγκεκριμένο τομέα του θέματος δεν υπάρχει καμία επιθυμία να είναι περιγραφικό. Κάποιος πρέπει να επιδιώξει να κυριαρχήσει σε όλες τις πτυχές που ασχολούνται ειδικά με το μυαλό. Η καθοδήγηση θα ήταν καλύτερη από το να προσπαθείς απλά να καταλάβεις κάτι που δεν είναι κατανοητό. Ο Σατανάς θέλει ο λαός του να μην είναι θύμα τα θύματα του να μην έχει αυτοέλεγχο ή έλεγχο σκέψης.

Κεφάλαιο (8): Η επιστολή του Σατανικού Πάπα (Πάπας-Jaheem R.Hilts)

Το Darkside έχει εξαίσια στην ανάπτυξη της νοημοσύνης, από την αρχαία διατύπωση του. Ο σατανικός τρόπος έχει υποστεί διακρίσεις λόγω της παρανόησης του Σατανά. Οι άνθρωποι μάλλον επαινούν ανθυγιεινές πράξεις κατά της ανθρωπότητας την αποδοχή λάθος από ορισμένους συνομηλίκους ή συγγενείς και συνοφρυώνομαι από θρησκευτικές πεποιθήσεις κάποιου άλλου. Για το μέλλον του Σατανικού όλοι οι Σατανικοί θα πρέπει να δείξουν τη διαφορά για να μειωθεί η άγνοια της αντίληψης του σατανικού πολιτισμού. Το μέλλον του Σατανικού θα ανθίσει στην ευτυχία σε όλες τις υποθέσεις του. Υπενθυμίστε στον εαυτό σας ξένους δεν έχει σημασία αν κάνετε το σωστό, ακόμη και κατ 'ιδίαν. Η ανάπτυξη του Σατανικού θα είναι μαζική και θα εφαρμόζεται προσεκτικά, ώστε οι άνθρωποι να μπορούν να δουν την αλήθεια αντί για ψεύτικο δόγμα. Μην επιτρέψετε στους λαούς άγνοια ή κρίση για να σας κάνει πραγματικότητα ερώτηση όταν προήλθε από την καθημερινή ψευδαισθήσεις τους / αυταπάτη.

Satanic Pope
(1220) **_Jaheem R. Hilts_**
May 9th, 2020 11:28pm (MST)

Κεφάλαιο (9): Σύντομη για το αόρατο κόσμο

Μια φορά κι έναν καιρό, σε έναν κόσμο που ασχολείται μόνο με τα πνεύματα, υπήρχε μια συνεχής δραστηριότητα στη χρήση υπερφυσικών ικανοτήτων στον αόρατο κόσμο. Όλα συνέβαιναν πνεύματα γεννούσαν πνεύματα. τα πνεύματα πέρασαν από τη διαδικασία του θανάτου ακόμα κι αν δεν μπορούσαν να πεθάνουν. Ο Θεός βασίλευε υπέρτατος και όλα φωτίστηκαν από το βασιλικό πνεύμα, τον Δημιουργό όλων των στην ύπαρξη. Το φως από το Θρόνο ήταν το φως του κόσμου. Ο Σατανάς γνώριζε περισσότερο από όλους στον πνευματικό κόσμο. Ήταν δάσκαλος και περνούσε χρόνο μελετώντας τα πράγματα που υπάρχουν. Η σκέψη πέρασε από το μυαλό του Θεού για ένα άλλο μέρος της δημιουργίας του. Ο Σατανάς ήταν γεμάτος χαρά, άρχισε να παίζει μουσική που ευχαριστούσε τον Θεό, οι Άγγελοι τραγούδησαν ακόμη. Τότε ο Θεός άρχισε να εκδηλώνει πράγματα στην ύπαρξη. Ο Σατανάς νόμιζε ότι ήταν μια επέκταση για τον αόρατο κόσμο. Ο Σατανάς είδε τη δόξα και την ομορφιά του Θεού, μπήκε στον πειρασμό να μιλήσει όταν είδε τον Θεό να σχηματίζει τον άνθρωπο, τότε περίμενε.........

(Θα συνεχιστεί)

Biblical Scholar
1220-*Jaheem R.Hilts*

Κεφάλαιο (10): Ο Σατανάς πρέπει να γίνεται κατανοητός και να μην αποφεύγει

Αν εξετάσουμε όλη τη βιβλική ιστορία η ανθρωπότητα έχει λάβει τις δικές του αποφάσεις από την επιβίωση στην ικανότητα. Λένε ότι "ο Εωσφόρος εκδιώχθηκε από τον Ουρανό" λένε "Ο Αδάμ και η Εύα εκδιώχθηκαν από τον Κήπο της Εδέμ". Δεν φταίει κανείς στο τέλος της μέρας. Ο Σατανάς δεν πρέπει να αποφεύγει ειδικά όταν κάποιος έχει γνώση του Σατανά, ακόμα κι αν κάποιος δεν το κάνει. Ο λόγος που το λέω αυτό είναι επειδή ο καθένας έχει μια επιλογή ελεύθερης θέλησης. Τι καλό θα ήταν να αποφύγεις κάποιον και έχεις την επιλογή να πάρεις μια απόφαση που κανείς δεν μπορεί να πάρει για σένα. Εμείς στο Σατανικό αγκαλιάζουμε τον Σατανά επειδή είναι γεμάτος σοφία που ο άνθρωπος δεν έχει καμία ικανότητα να έχει. Έχουμε την παραμικρή εικόνα για τον κόσμο που δεν έχει δει. Ο Σατανάς είναι μια διαφορετική μορφή δημιουργίας. εκείνοι που μυήθηκαν μπορούν να κατανοήσουν την ευρύτητα του πώς να επικοινωνούν και να κατανοήσουν τι αντιμετωπίζουν. Ο Σατανάς πρέπει να γίνεται κατανοητός και να μην αποφεύγει. (1220)

Κεφάλαιο (11): Η είσοδος είναι σημαντική

Είναι σημαντικό να γνωρίζουμε ότι η είσοδος στον Σατανικό είναι ευαίσθητη, πολύ λεπτή. Θα πρέπει να είναι ένα θέμα που λαμβάνεται πολύ σοβαρά υπόψη και δεν επιτρέπεται να γίνεται κατάχρηση. Είναι ένας κόσμος μέσα σε έναν κόσμο, η γνώση δεν πρέπει να πάει χαμένη. Οι περισσότεροι άνθρωποι δεν θα αναζητήσουν την αλήθεια και η περιέργεια είναι κοινή. Η σημασία είναι πέρα από την κατανόηση των αμύητων. Εκείνοι με γνώση μπορεί να θέλουν να προωθήσουν την πνευματική ανάπτυξη. πρακτική του πολιτισμού της σατανικής ενότητας. Πώς κάποιος έρχεται προς τα εμπρός με την ικανότητα να αναπτυχθούν είναι σημαντική, η αγάπη για το Σατανικό πρέπει να είναι ισχυρή σε μία εξάσκηση μυήσεις σε άλλους ή αποτυχία είναι δυνατή. Καθώς το φως λάμπει στο σκοτάδι και το σκοτάδι λάμπει στο φως, όλα θα είναι. Ποτέ μην επιδιώκουν να κάνουν το μυαλό κάποιου άλλου μέχρι παράδοση / υποβολή είναι για όλους τους μαθητές.

Übersetzt ins Deutsche
German

Die kenntnisreichsten werden wissen, dass Satan schon länger da ist als die Menschheit. Das Missverständnis aus dem individuellen Verständnis einer Person eliminiert Nachsicht in höhere Anerkennung. Der Geist kann nur in der Finsternis sehen, man muss die verbotene Wahrheit gelehrt werden, um sich in einer Reise auszuzeichnen, die in allen Augen notwendig ist, besonders das 3. Auge. Satan hat geheimnisse des Himmels und der Erde denen offenbart, die ihm am vertrauenswürdigsten sind; seine Begründung, eine Erklärung abzugeben. Um an die Hilfe Satans zu glauben, akzeptiert sie teilweise, dass sogar Satan ein Teil der ganzen Schöpfung ist. Warum wird man auf das herabschauen, was sie nicht verstehen? Entschuldigungen für ihre Taten. Satan spielt eine Rolle in den Dingen, die auf der Erde geschehen; einige sind angenehm, andere als Lektion. Danke satan dafür, dass er dich stärker gemacht hat, gib dich nicht auf. (1220)

Kapitel (1): Satan ist uralt

Von Anfang der Zeit lange bevor das Bewusstsein überhaupt eine Option war, existierte Satan. Das Universum war nur voller Geister; andere Dinge, die nur in der unsichtbaren Welt fähig waren. Intelligenz würde nicht einmal auf menschlicher Ebene verstanden werden, weil Menschen nicht existierten, außer in einem zukünftigen Plan. Die Aktivitäten in diesen spirituellen Bereichen waren nie in der Lage, dokumentationen. Satan war vor der Kreativität und strukturellen Entwicklung von architektonischen Entwürfen von vergangenen Generationen der Menschheit. Satan ist uralt, weil wir seine Existenzzeit nicht berechnen können, als er geboren oder geformt wurde. Wir werden erkennen, dass diejenigen in biblischen Zeiten Satan für Weisheit und die Fähigkeit, weiter als andere zu sehen. Satan ist kein Narr, wir alle haben Entscheidungen Satans Wahl war großartig in seinen Augen. Richtig und falsch sind nur durch die eine Wahrnehmung, Sündigungen haben täglich unzähligen Menschen Glück gebracht, länger als anerkannt. Satan muss nicht für euch denken, ihr seid ein Teil des Anfangs, egal wie viel Zeit vergeht.

Kapitel (2): Wie man Satan hilft

Ihr müsst erkennen, dass ihr Satan hilft, dass es euch hilft. Satan wird wollen, dass ihr alle Freuden und Wünsche habt, die ihr für euch selbst wollt. Indem ihr Satan hilft, werdet ihr alle Sünden in der Welt wiedergutmachen. Ihr helfe Satan, indem ihr anderen helst; Menschen kommen zusammen und genießen die Zeit miteinander auf Satans weisen, während Sünde schön ist, müssen Sie ihre Schönheit verbreiten. Satan zu helfen sollte nicht als Schwäche betrachtet werden, auch wenn die Menschen das Werk mit Stirnrunzeln begehen werden. Ihr könnt Satan helfen, indem ihr nicht töricht seid, indem ihr mit gutem Beispiel vorangeht und mehr Frieden schafft als diejenigen, die sich als gottgegeben bekennen. Ihr könnt Satan helfen, indem ihr loyal und vertrauenswürdig gegenüber der Satansarmee seid. Es gibt einen Kampf zwischen Gut und Böse und Satan will nicht nur für das Böse bekannt sein; Zerstörung.

Kapitel (3): Konvertiten zum Satan

Ich würde niemandem raten, zu versuchen, Satan selbst zu verstehen. Es wäre größer, den Dunklen Mächten vorgestellt zu werden. Man kann die Hoffnung verlieren, ohne Einweihung auf Satan zuzugehen. Die Fähigkeit, sich zu bekehren, ist wie alles andere, man muss Glauben haben. Der Glaube an Satan mag nicht für jeden leicht sein wegen des negativen Klatsches, der Aufnahmen falscher Interpretationen. Geist, Körper und Seele müssen darin sein, um Vollendung zu erhalten; nichts fehlt etwas Wichtiges. Die Bekehrung zum Satan ist sensibel, weil es zumindest den anfänglichen Prozess geheimnisvoll ist, es ist sehr vorteilhaft für diejenigen, die dazu bestimmt sind, sich aus ihren vergangenen Verwirrungen zu bekehren. Ich könnte auf andere Bücher verweisen, um das Verständnis für dieses Thema zu erweitern. Ich entscheide mich dafür, weil sie Sie beim Konvertieren nicht unterstützen. Satan steht für verbotenes Wissen oder geheimes Wissen. Wenn ihr euch zum Satan bekehrt, müsst ihr anfangen, euch zu entwickeln, nachdem ihr die Samen getragen habt. Sie werden wachsen, auch wenn Sie sich selbst widerstehen.

Wenn man sich zum Satan bekehrt, ist es ein Neuanfang, ein Leben ohne Reue, wenn man Wissen und Weisheit liebt.

Kapitel (4): Beziehungen & Satan

Wahre Liebe findet man leicht in zwei Menschen, die zusammen sein wollen, basierend auf Vertrauen. Es ist nichts, was aus einer unbewussten Entscheidung gemacht wird, beide werden das gleiche wollen müssen. Das verbotene Wissen, das an den Eingeweihten weitergegeben wird, reicht aus, um mit einer Beziehungssituation umzugehen. Es gibt eine Verbindung, die nicht beschrieben werden kann, die Welt wird als angenehmer visualisiert. Es gibt keine Ungewissheit, die eindringen kann, nichts Unbekanntes, das euch ein Teil brechen kann, unter Bezugnahme auf (Dark Forces Energy). Satan ist großartig darin, sein Volk in ehrfürchtigen Beziehungen zu halten, die beide den Weg Satans bereisen. Satan kann auch bei guten Beziehungen, wenn einer seiner Nachfolger ist, in einer Beziehung mit jemandem mit einem anderen Glauben festgestellt werden. Wie gesagt, dass Satan uralt ist, so gibt es keine Theorie, die Satan über die Liebe weiß. Es steht außer Frage, dass diejenigen, die sich auf dem Satanspfad befinden, Einander lieben werden, das ist natürlich, wenn sie es wollen. Eine Beziehung, die mit der Einweihung gegründet wurde, ist ein gesegnetes Wildfeuer, das an einem sicheren Ort eingepfert ist. Emotionen beeinflussen den freien Willen und umgekehrt keine Aufgabe für die Schwachen.

Kapitel (5): Weise Poesie Satans

Wenn sie nur nicht missverstanden würden, wie hell wird das Leuchten vom Himmel sein? Als die Formulierung des Wassers in den Augen meines bloßen Auges meinen Geist in die Antike führt, erscheint ihr in Herrlichkeit. Die Welt ist eine Reflexion, eurer Existenz. Die Gedanken sind mit unauffälligen Freuden erfüllt. Ich sehe deine Schönheit, ich will dein Unternehmen, und ich weiß, dass du nicht naiv bin. Durch die Wolken, wenn sie mich auf ihnen stehen halten können. Ich werde die Strecke zurücklegen; Ich werde verankern, nichts außer unendlich zu besetzen.

1220 (Gedichte)

Kapitel (6): Gemeinschaft Satans

Im Laufe der Jahrhunderte gab es Gemeinschaften, die vom Satan getrieben wurden. Nur weil eine Person sich entscheidet, dem verbotenen Wissen und der Weisheit Satans zu folgen, macht sie nicht weniger als jeder andere, der den Planeten Erde teilt. Eine Gemeinschaft Satans ist eine Gemeinschaft, die sich mit Ritualen beschäftigt. Sie befassen sich damit, Dinge vorherzusehen, bevor sie geschehen, und gut vorbereitet zu sein. Es wäre eine Ehre, überhaupt in die Aktivitäten einer solchen Gemeinschaft aufgenommen zu werden, während andere es vielleicht anders sehen. Seht, wie alt die Erde und die verschiedenen Energien sind; die meisten Menschen nehmen nur zu Fuß nach draußen oder öffnen ein Fenster im Haus. Wenn man mit der Weisheit und dem Wissen umgeht, die man von Satan bekommen kann, findet man viel Glück, Selbstzufriedenheit, die selbst in einer Grundform gut ist, weil das Lernen nie aufhört. Die Gemeinschaft Satans sollte niemals verworfen werden, weil sie anbietet, Intelligenz anzuwenden, wo sie sein muss. Intelligenz zu verstehen ist auch für ein Mitglied des Satanspfades üblich.

Kapitel (7): Wie kann Satan euch helfen?

Es ist wichtig zu wissen, dass wir alle einen Kopf voller Gedanken haben und mehr in Zeiten unterschiedlicher Emotionen erscheinen. Für die Menschen, die vom Satanspfad leben, sind sie mit diesem täglichen Ereignis im Geist vertraut. Sie haben sich so genau studiert, dass sie ihre Gedanken wie mit ihren Händen auswählen können, anstatt die Wahl der Handlung. Satan spielt eine wichtige Rolle in dieser Fähigkeit, weil es irgendwann ermutigt wird, wenn er sich dem Satan-Volk anschließt. Dieses Kapitel berührt das Bewusstsein für einen bestimmten Themenbereich, es gibt keinen Wunsch, beschreibend zu sein. Man muss versuchen, sich in allen Aspekten zu beherrschen, besonders im Umgang mit dem Geist. Anleitung wäre besser, als einfach etwas zu verstehen, was nicht verständlich ist. Satan möchte, dass sein Volk nicht Opfer von nicht selbstbeherrschmlichen oder Gedankenkontrolle wird.

Kapitel (8): Der Brief des satanischen Papstes (Papst-Jaheem R.Hilts)

Die Darkside ist seit ihrer uralten Formulierung exquisit in der Entwicklung von Intelligenz. Der satanische Weg wurde wegen des Missverständnisses Satans diskriminiert. Die Menschen loben vielmehr ungesunde Handlungen, wenn die Menschheit von bestimmten Gleichaltrigen oder Verwandten Unrecht akzeptiert und den religiösen Glauben eines anderen mit Stirnrunzeln übergeht. Für die Zukunft des Satanischen sollten alle Satanischen den Unterschied zeigen, um die Unwissenheit der Wahrnehmung der satanischen Kultur zu verringern. Die Zukunft des Satanischen wird in all seinen Angelegenheiten im Glück gedeihen. Erinnern Sie sich an Außenstehende, egal ob Sie es auch privat tun. Das Wachstum des Satanischen wird massiv und sorgfältig angewendet werden, damit die Menschen die Wahrheit sehen können, anstatt falschedogische. Lasst nicht zu, dass Die Unwissenheit oder das Urteilsvermögen der

Völker euch die Realität in Frage stellt, wenn sie aus ihren täglichen Illusionen/Wahnvorstellungen kam.

Satanic Pope
(1220) **Jaheem R.Hilts**
May 9th, 2020 11:28pm (MST)

Kapitel (9): Kurz über die unsichtbare Welt

Es war einmal, in einer Welt, die nur mit Geistern zu tun hatte, gab es eine ständige Aktivität, übernatürliche Fähigkeiten in der unsichtbaren Welt zu nutzen. Alles, was geschah, Geister gebären Geister; Geister durchliefen den Prozess des Sterbens, obwohl sie nicht sterben konnten. Gott herrschte über die Oberhand und alles wurde vom königlichen Geist erleuchtet, dem Schöpfer aller Inexistenz. Das Licht von The Throne war das Licht der Welt. Satan war mehr bedienbar als alle in der geistigen Welt. Er war ein Meister und er verbrachte Zeit damit, über die Dinge nachzudenken, die es gibt. Der Gedanke ging Gottes Geist für einen anderen Teil seiner Schöpfung. Satan war voller Freude, er an, Musik zu spielen, die Gott gefiel, die Engel sangen sogar. Dann Gott an, Dinge in der Existenz zu manifestieren. Satan dachte, es sei eine Erweiterung für die unsichtbare Welt. Satan sah Gottes Herrlichkeit und Schönheit, er war versucht zu sprechen, als er sah, wie Gott den Menschen formte, dann wartete er........

(Fortsetzung)

Biblical Scholar
<u>1220</u>-*Jaheem R. Hilts*

Kapitel (10): Satan sollte verstanden und nicht gemieden werden

Wenn wir uns die ganze biblische Geschichte ansehen, hat die Menschheit ihre eigenen Entscheidungen vom Überleben bis zur Fähigkeit getroffen. Sie sagen " Lucifer wurde aus dem Himmel geworfen" sie sagen "Adam und Eva wurden aus dem Garten Eden geworfen". Am Ende des Tages gibt es niemanden, der schuld ist. Satan sollte nicht gemieden werden, besonders wenn man Satan kennt, auch wenn man es nicht tut. Der Grund, warum ich dies sage, ist, dass jeder eine freie Wahl hat. Was nützt es, jemanden zu meiden, und Sie haben die Wahl, eine Entscheidung zu treffen, die niemand für Sie treffen kann. Wir in Der Satanische umarmen Satan, weil er von Weisheit erfüllt ist, die der Mensch nicht haben kann. Wir haben den geringsten Einblick in die ganze unsichtbare Welt. Satan ist eine andere Form der Schöpfung; Die Eingeweihten können die Breite der Kommunikation verstehen und verstehen, womit sie es zu tun haben. Satan sollte verstanden und nicht gemieden werden. (1220)

Kapitel (11): Der Eingang ist wichtig

Es ist wichtig zu wissen, dass der Eingang in das Satanische sensibel, sehr heikel ist. Es sollte eine Angelegenheit sein, die sehr ernst genommen wird und nicht missbraucht werden darf. Es ist eine Welt in einer Welt, Wissen sollte nicht verschwendet werden. Die meisten Menschen werden nicht die Wahrheit suchen und Neugier ist üblich. Die Bedeutung ist für uneingeweihte Uneingeweihte unverständlich. Diejenigen, die Wissen haben, möchten vielleicht das spirituelle Wachstum fördern; die Kultur der satanischen Einheit zu praktizieren. Wie man mit der Fähigkeit zum Wachsen kommt, ist wichtig, die Liebe zum Satanischen muss stark sein in einem, der Einweihungen an anderen praktiziert, oder Scheitern ist möglich. Wenn lichtinstes Licht in Dunkelheit und Dunkelheit im Licht scheint, wird es alles sein. Versuchen Sie nie, jemand anderen Geist bis Kapitulation / Unterwerfung ist für alle Studenten.

Isinalin sa Pilipino
Filipino

Malalaman ng karamihan na alam na mas matagal si Satanas kaysa sa sangkatauhan. Ang hindi pagkakaunawaan ng taong may pag-unawa sa isang tao ay nag-aalis ng kasiyahan sa mas mataas na pagkilala. Makikita lamang sa kadiliman ang Espiritu, kailangang ituro sa isang tao ang ipinagbabawal na katotohanan upang humusay sa paglalakbay na kinakailangan sa lahat ng mata lalo na sa 3rd mata. Inihayag ni Satanas ang mga lihim ng langit at lupa sa mga taong mapagkakatiwalaan niya; ang layunin niyang gumawa ng pahayag. Para maniwala sa tulong ni Satanas, bahagyang tinatanggap na maging si Satanas ay bahagi ng buong paglikha. Bakit titingnan ng isang tao ang hindi nila nauunawaan? Mga pagdadahilan sa kanilang mga kilos. Si Satanas ay may papel na ginagampanan sa mga bagay na nagaganap sa lupa; ang ilan ay kasiya-siya, ang ilan ay isang aral.

Magpasalamat kay Satanas para sa paggawa ninyo nang mas malakas, huwag sumuko sa inyong sarili. (1220)

Kabanata (1): si Satanas ay noong unang

Mula sa simula ng panahon bago pa man ang kabatiran ay naging isang opsiyon, si Satanas ay umiral. Ang sansinukob ay puno lamang ng mga Espiritu; iba pang mga bagay na may kakayahan lamang sa mga hindi nakikitang mundo. Ang katalinuhan ay hindi rin mauunawaan sa antas ng tao dahil ang mga tao ay hindi umiiral, maliban sa isang plano sa hinaharap. Ang mga aktibidad sa espirituwal na mga ito ay hindi kailanman nagkaroon ng mga dokumento. Si Satanas ay nasa harap ng pagkamalikhain at istruktura na pagbuo ng mga disenyo ng arkitektura ng mga nakaraang henerasyon ng sangkatauhan. Si Satanas ay noong unang panahon dahil hindi natin kayang makalkula ang kanyang oras sa buhay, kapag siya ay ipinanganak o nabuo. Malalaman natin na kasama sa mga panahon ng Biblia ang sumapi kay Satanas para sa karunungan at kakayahang makakita pa kaysa sa iba. Si Satanas ay hindi hangal tayong lahat ay pumipili ng pasiya ni Satanas na kahanga-hanga sa kanyang mga mata. Ang tama at mali ay sa pamamagitan lamang ng pagkaunawa, ang pagkakasala ay nagdulot ng kaligayahan sa napakaraming tao araw-araw, na mas matagal kaysa kinilala. Hindi na kayo kailangang isipin ni Satanas, kayo ay bahagi ng simula, kahit gaano karami ang oras na dulot nito.

Kabanata (2): Paano tulungan si Satanas

Kailangan ninyong matanto na tinutulungan ninyo si Satanas para tulungan kayo. Nais ni Satanas na magkaroon kayo ng lahat ng kasiyahan at hangaring nais ninyo para sa inyong sarili. Sa pagtulong kay Satanas ay makagagawa kayo ng kabutihan sa lahat ng kasalanan sa mundo. Tinutulungan ninyo si Satanas sa pamamagitan ng pagtulong sa kapwa; ang mga tao ay magkakasamang dumarating at nagtatamasa ng panahon sa bawat isa sa mga paraan ni Satanas, samantalang maganda ang kasalanan, kailangan ninyong palaganapin ang kagandahan nito. Ang pagtulong kay Satanas ay hindi dapat ituring na kahinaan, kahit na ang mga tao ay pagsimangot sa gawain. Matutulungan ninyo si Satanas sa pamamagitan ng hindi pagiging mangmang sa pamumuno sa pamamagitan ng halimbawa, paglikha ng higit na kapayapaan kaysa mga nagsasabing na makadiyos. Matutulungan ninyo si Satanas sa pagiging matapat at mapagkakatiwalaan sa hukbo ni Satanas. May digmaan sa pagitan ng mabuti at masama at ni Satanas ay hindi lamang nais na makilala para sa kasamaan; pagkawasak.

Kabanata (3): Gabay kay Satanas

Hindi ko pinapayuhan ang isang tao na subukan at unawain si Satanas nang mag-isa. Mas mainam na ipakilala ito sa mga madilim na pwersa. Maaaring mawalan ng pag-asa ang isang tao sa pagsisikap na tulungan si Satanas nang walang pagsisimula. Ang kakayahang maging convert ay tulad ng iba pa, kailangan mong manampalataya. Ang pananampalataya kay Satanas ay hindi maaaring madali para sa lahat dahil sa mga negatibong tsismis, mga inirekord ng maling interpretasyon. Isip, katawan at kaluluwa ay dapat na ito upang makatanggap ng pagtatapos; wala nang ibang bagay na mahalaga. Ang pag-convert kay Satanas ay sensitibo dahil ito ay malihim sa unang proseso ng hindi bababa sa, ito ay lubos na kapaki-pakinabang para sa mga na nakatalaga sa convert mula sa kanilang nakaraang confusions. Maaari kong banggitin ang iba pang mga aklat para magpapalawak ang pag-unawa sa paksang ito. Pinipili ko hindi dahil sa hindi nila kayo masusuportahan. Si Satanas ay kumakatawan sa ipinagbabawal na kaalaman o lihim na kaalaman. Sa pamamagitan ng pag-convert kay Satanas, kailangang magsimula, matapos dalhin ang mga binhi. Lalago sila kahit na malalabanan mo ang iyong sarili. Ang pag-convert kay Satanas ito ay bagong simula, isang buhay na walang panghihinayang, kung gusto ninyo ng kaalaman at karunungan.

Kabanata (4): mga ugnayan & kay Satanas

Ang tunay na pagmamahal ay madaling makita sa dalawang tao na gustong magkasama-sama, batay sa pagtitiwala. Ito ay hindi anumang ginawa ng isang walang malay desisyon parehong ay may upang gusto ang parehong bagay. Ang ipinagbabawal na kaalaman na kung saan ay naipasa sa ang simulan ay sapat na sa paghawak ng isang relasyon sitwasyon. Mayroong isang koneksyon na hindi maaaring ilarawan ang mundo ay nakinita bilang mas kasiya-siya. Walang kawalang-katiyakan na maaaring tumagos, walang hindi kilala na maaaring masira sa iyo ng isang bahagi, na tumutukoy sa (madilim pwersa enerhiya). Dakila si Satanas sa pagsunod sa kanyang mga tao sa kahanga-hangang relasyon, kapwa sa paglalakbay sa landas ni Satanas. Maaari ding maging malinaw si Satanas sa pagkakaroon ng mabubuting ugnayan, kapag ang isa sa kanyang mga tagasunod ay, sa pakikipag-ugnayan sa isang taong iba ang relihiyon. Tulad ng nakasaad sa unang salita si Satanas ay walang teoriya na alam ni Satanas ang tungkol sa pagmamahal. Walang alinlangang ang mga nasa landas ng Satanas ay magkakaroon ng pag-ibig sa isa 't isa, mangyari pa ito kung gusto nila. Isang relasyon na itinatag sa pagsisimula, ay isang pinagpala ligaw na apoy containe ...

Kabanata (5): matalinong tula ni Satanas

Kung ikaw lamang ay hindi hindi naunawaan, gaano maliwanag ang ningning mula sa kalangitan? Habang ang pagbabalangkas ng tubig sa paningin ng aking hubad na mata ay humantong sa aking isipan sa sinaunang panahon, kayo ay nagpakita sa kaluwalhatian. Ang mundo ay isang salamin, ng inyong pag-iral. Ang mga kaisipan ay puno ng hindi pangkaraniwang kasiyahan. Nakikita ko ang iyong kagandahan, gusto ko ang iyong kumpanya, at alam kong hindi maging walang alam. Sa kabila ng mga ulap, kung mahawakan nila akong nakatayo sa kanila. Maglalakbay ako nang malayo; Wala akong sumasakop maliban sa walang hanggan.

1220 (tula)

Kabanata (6): Community of Satanas

Sa mga edad na may mga komunidad na pinalayas ni Satanas. Dahil lamang sa pinipili ng isang tao na sundin ang ipinagbabawal na kaalaman at karunungan ni Satanas ay hindi sila gawing mas mababa kaysa iba pang pagbabahagi ng planeta na mundo. Ang komunidad ni Satanas ay isang komunidad na may mga ritwal. Nakikitungo sila sa mga nakinitang bagay bago sila mangyari at maging handa. Ito ay isang karangalang maging isang karangalan na maging tanggapin sa mga gawain ng tulad ng isang komunidad, habang ang iba ay maaaring makita ito iba't-ibang. Tingnan kung gaano na luma ang mundo at ang iba 't ibang lakas; impluwensya karamihan sa mga tao ay naglalakad lang sa labas o nagbubukas ng bintana sa bahay. Kapag ang pagharap sa karunungan at kaalaman ay maaaring magmula kay Satanas, makakakita kayo ng maraming kaligayahan, kasiyahan sa sarili, na kahit sa isang mahalagang anyo ay mabuti dahil ang pag-aaral ay hindi tumitigil. Hindi dapat itinapon ang komunidad ni Satanas dahil nag-aalok sila na mag-aplay ng katalinuhan kung saan ito kailangang maging. Ang maunawaan katalinuhan ay karaniwang para sa kahit isang miyembro ng landas ng Satanas. (1220)

Kabanata (7): Paano makokontrol ang inyong mga iniisip ang makatutulong sa inyo ni Satanas?

Mahalagang malaman na lahat tayo ay may ulo na puno ng kaisipan at mas lumilitaw sa oras ng iba 't ibang emosyon. Para sa mga taong namumuhay ayon sa landas ng Satanas, pamilyar sila sa pang-araw-araw na pangyayaring ito sa loob ng isipan. Napag-aralan nila ang kanilang sarili sa punto na maaari nilang piliin ang kanilang mga iniisip tulad ng paggamit ng kanilang kamay, sa halip na pagpili ng aksyon. Mahalaga ang ginampanan ni Satanas sa kakayahang ito dahil ito ay hinihikayat sa ilang sandali nang sumapi sa mga tao ni Satanas. Ang kabanatang ito ay nakaaantig sa kamalayan ng isang partikular na lugar ng paksa na walang nais na ilarawan. Dapat hangarin ng isang tao na maging amo sa lahat ng aspeto lalo na sa pag-iisip. Ang patnubay ay higit pa sa pagsisikap na maunawaan lang ang isang bagay na hindi naiintindihan. Gusto ni Satanas na hindi maging biktima ng hindi pagkakaroon ng kontrol o pag-iisip ang kanyang mga tao.

Kabanata (8): ang sulat mula sa ni Satanas Pope (Pope-Jaheem R. Hilts)

Ang Darkside ay katangi-tangi sa pag-unlad ng katalinuhan, dahil nito sinaunang pagbabalangkas. Ang ni Satanas paraan ay nadiskrimina dahil sa maling pagkaunawa ni Satanas. Ang mga tao sa halip purihin ang masama ang kilos sa sangkatauhan ay tumatanggap ng mali mula sa ilang mga kabarkada o kamag-anak at pagsimangot sa paniniwala ng ibang tao sa relihiyon. Para sa hinaharap ng ni Satanas ang lahat ng ni Satanas ay dapat magpakita ng pagkakaiba upang mabawasan ang kamangmangan ng pang-unawa ng ni Satanas kultura. Ang kinabukasan ng ni Satanas ay mananagana sa kaligayahan sa lahat ng gawain nito. Paalalahanan ang iyong mga tagalabas ay hindi mahalaga kung tama ang iyong ginagawa, kahit na sa mga pribado. Ang paglago ng mga ni Satanas ay dapat na malaki at maingat na inilapat upang makita ng mga tao ang katotohanan sa halip na maling sa doktrina. Huwag payagan ang mga tao na hindi sang-ayon o manghusga na gawin mong totoo ito kapag nagmula ito sa araw-araw na ilusyon/panlilinlang.

Satanic Pope
(1220) **_Jaheem R.Hilts_**
May 9th, 2020 11:28pm (MST)

Kabanata (9): maikling isipin ang daigdig na hindi nakikita

Minsan, sa isang mundo lamang na nakikitungo sa mga Espiritu, laging may aktibidad sa paggamit ng hindi pangkaraniwang mga kakayahan sa mundong hindi nakikita. Lahat ng nangyayari sa Espiritu ay pagsilang ng mga Espiritu; nagpunta ang mga Espiritu sa proseso ng kamatayan kahit na hindi sila mamamatay. Ang Diyos ay naghari at lahat ay naliwanagan ng maharlikang Espiritu, ang lumikha ng lahat ng nasa buhay. Ang liwanag mula sa trono ay ang ilaw ng sanlibutan. Mas alam ni Satanas ang lahat sa espirituwal na daigdig. Siya ay isang guro at nag-ukol siya ng panahon sa pagninilay sa mga bagay na may buhay. Ang kaisipang ito ay tumawid sa isipan ng Diyos para sa isa pang bahagi ng kanyang paglikha. Si Satanas ay puspos ng kagalakan, siya ay nagsimulang tumugtog ng musika na nalugod sa Diyos, ang mga anghel ay kumanta pa. Pagkatapos ay nagsimulang nagpapatunay ang Diyos sa mga bagay na may buhay. Inisip ni Satanas na ang paglawak ng mundong hindi nakikita. Nakita ni Satanas ang kaluwalhatian at kagandahan ng Diyos, siya ay tinukso na magsalita nang makita niya ang Diyos na bumubuo ng tao, pagkatapos siya ay naghintay ...

(Upang ipagpatuloy)

Biblical Scholar

1220-*Jaheem R.Hilts*

Kabanata (10): si Satanas ay dapat maunawaan at hindi Ikinait

Kung titingnan natin ang buong kasaysayan ng Biblia, ang sangkatauhan ay nakagawa ng sarili niyang desisyon mula sa kaligtasan upang magkaroon ng kakayahan. Sabi nila "si Lucifer ay umahon mula sa Langit" sabi nila "sina Adan at Eva ay casted mula sa Halamanan ng Eden". Walang sinuman ang sisihin sa katapusan ng araw. Si Satanas ay hindi dapat Ikinait lalo na kapag ang isang tao ay may kaalaman tungkol kay Satanas, kahit na hindi isa. Ang dahilan kung bakit sinasabi ko ito ay dahil ang lahat ay may freewill pagpipilian. Anong kabutihan ang dapat iwasan ang isang tao at ikaw ay may pagpiling gumawa ng isang desisyon na walang magagawa para sa iyo. Tinatanggap natin sa ni Satanas si Satanas dahil puspos siya ng karunungan na walang kakayahang magkaroon ang tao. May ilan tayong kabatiran sa buong mundo na hindi nakikita. Si Satanas ay ibang uri ng paglikha; ang mga pinasimulan ay maaaring maunawaan ang lapad kung paano makipag-usap at maunawaan kung ano ang kanilang pakikitungo sa. Dapat maunawaan at hindi Ikinait si Satanas. (1220)

Kabanata (11): ang pasukan ay mahalaga

Mahalagang malaman na ang pagpasok sa ni Satanas ay sensitibo, lubhang maselan. Dapat maging seryoso at hindi pinapayagang abusuhin ang isang bagay. Ito ay isang mundo sa loob ng mundo, ang kaalaman ay hindi dapat mawasak. Karamihan sa mga tao ay hindi maghahangad na ang katotohanan at pag-uusisa ay karaniwan. Ang kahalagahan ay hindi kayang unawain ang uninitiated. Ang mga may kaalaman ay maaaring naisin sa karagdagang espirituwal na pag-unlad; Praktisin ang kultura ng ni Satanas pagkakaisa. Kung paano ang isa ay dumating sa paglakad na may kakayahan upang lumago ay mahalaga, ang pag-ibig para sa ni Satanas ay dapat na matatag sa isang pagsasanay initiations sa iba o kabiguan ay posible. Tulad ng liwanag na nagliliwanag sa kadiliman at kadiliman sa liwanag, lahat ay mangyayari. Huwag kailanman hangaring gawing iba ang isipan ng ibang tao para isuko/isumite sa lahat ng estudyante.

Traduit en Français
French

118

Les plus compétents sauront que Satan existe depuis plus longtemps que l'humanité. L'incompréhension de la compréhension individuelle d'une personne élimine l'indulgence dans une reconnaissance plus élevée. L'esprit ne peut voir que dans les ténèbres, il faut apprendre à la vérité interdite d'exceller dans un voyage nécessaire à tous les yeux, en particulier au 3ème œil. Satan a révélé des secrets du Ciel et de la Terre à ceux qui lui sont les plus dignes de confiance ; sa cause de faire une déclaration. Croire en l'aide de Satan, c'est en partie accepter que même Satan fait partie de toute la création. Pourquoi regardera-t-on en bas de ce qu'ils ne comprennent pas? Trouver des excuses pour leurs actions. Satan a un rôle dans les choses qui se déroulent sur Terre; certains sont agréables, d'autres comme une leçon.

Remerciez Satan de vous avoir rendu plus fort, ne vous abandonnez pas. (1220)

Chapitre (1): Satan est ancien

Dès le début des temps bien avant même que la conscience ne soit une option, Satan existait. L'univers était plein d'esprits; d'autres choses qui n'étaient capables que dans le monde invisible. L'intelligence ne serait même pas comprise sur le plan humain parce que les humains n'existaient pas, sauf dans un plan futur. Les activités dans ces royaumes spirituels n'ont jamais été capables de documentation. Satan était avant la créativité et le développement structurel des conceptions architecturales par les générations passées de l'humanité. Satan est ancien parce que nous ne pouvons pas calculer son temps dans l'existence, quand il est né ou formé. Nous saurons que ceux de l'époque biblique ont rejoint Satan pour la sagesse et la capacité de voir plus loin que les autres. Satan n'est pas un imbécile, nous avons tous le choix de Satan était magnifique dans ses yeux. Le bien et le mal ne sont que par la perception, le péché a apporté le bonheur à d'innombrables quantités de personnes par jour, plus longtemps que reconnu. Satan n'a pas à penser pour vous, vous êtes une partie du début, peu importe ho ...

Chapitre (2): Comment aider Satan

Tu dois réaliser que tu aides Satan, ça t'aide. Satan voudra que vous ayez tous les plaisirs et les désirs que vous voulez pour vous-même. En aidant Satan, vous allez faire bon de tous les péchés dans le monde. Vous aidez Satan en aidant les autres; les gens se réunissent et profiter du temps les uns avec les autres dans les façons de Satan, tandis que le péché est beau, vous devez répandre sa beauté. Aider Satan ne doit pas être considéré comme une faiblesse, même si les gens fronceront les sourcils sur le travail. Vous pouvez aider Satan en n'étant pas stupide en menant l'exemple, créant plus de paix que ceux qui prétendent être pieux. Vous pouvez aider Satan en étant loyal et digne de confiance à l'Armée Satan. Il y a une bataille entre le bien et le mal et Satan

ne veut pas seulement être connu pour le
mal ; Destruction.

Chapitre (3): Convertir à Satan

Je ne conseillerais pas à quelqu'un d'essayer de comprendre Satan par lui-même. Il serait plus grand d'être introduit dans les Forces obscures. On peut perdre espoir en essayant de tendre la main à Satan sans initiation. La capacité de convertir est comme tout le reste, vous devez avoir la foi. La foi en Satan n'est peut-être pas facile pour tout le monde à cause des commérages négatifs, des enregistrements de fausses interprétations. L'esprit, le corps et l'âme doivent être en elle pour recevoir l'achèvement; rien ne manque quelque chose d'important. Convertir à Satan est sensible parce que c'est secret le processus initial au moins, il est très bénéfique pour ceux qui sont destinés à convertir de leurs confusions passées. Je pourrais faire référence à d'autres livres pour élargir la compréhension de ce sujet. Je choisis de ne pas le faire parce qu'ils ne vous soutiendront pas la conversion. Satan représente la connaissance interdite ou la connaissance secrète. Se convertir à Satan, vous devez commencer à développer, après avoir porté les graines. Ils grandiront même si vous vous résistez vous-même. Convertir à Satan c'est un nouveau départ, un ...

Chapitre (4) : Relations et Satan

Le véritable amour se trouve facilement chez deux personnes qui veulent être ensemble, sur la base de la confiance. Ce n'est pas quelque chose fait sur une décision inconsciente à la fois devra vouloir la même chose. La connaissance interdite qui est transmise à l'initié est suffisante pour gérer une situation relationnelle. Il ya un lien qui ne peut pas être décrit le monde est visualisé comme plus agréable. Il n'y a pas d'incertitude qui peut pénétrer, rien d'inconnu qui peut vous briser une partie, se référant à (Dark Forces Energy). Satan est grand en gardant son peuple dans des relations impressionnantes, les deux voyageant le chemin de Satan. Satan peut également être noté en faisant de bonnes relations, quand l'un de ses disciples est, dans une relation avec quelqu'un d'une foi différente. Comme indiqué avant Satan est ancien il n'y a donc aucune théorie que Satan connaît sur l'amour. Il ne fait aucun doute que ceux sur le chemin Satan auront l'amour les uns avec les autres, c'est bien sûr s'ils le veulent. Une relation fondée avec l'initiation, est un feu sauvage béni contenir ...Chapter

(5): Poésie sage de Satan

Si seulement vous n'étiez pas mal compris, quelle sera la lueur du ciel? Comme la formulation de l'eau à la vue de mon œil nu conduit mon esprit vers les temps anciens, vous apparaissez dans la gloire. Le monde est un reflet.de votre existence. Les pensées sont remplies de plaisirs ordinaires. Je vois ta beauté, je veux ta compagnie, et je sais que je ne suis pas naïf. A travers les nuages, s'ils peuvent me tenir debout sur eux. Je vais parcourir la distance; Je vais ancrer n'occuper rien d'autre qu'infini.

1220 (Poésie)

Chapitre (6): Communauté de Satan

Au fil des âges, il y a eu des communautés qui ont été animées par Satan. Ce n'est pas parce qu'une personne choisit de suivre la connaissance et la sagesse interdites de Satan qu'elle ne les rend pas moins que quiconque partageant la planète Terre. Une communauté de Satan est une communauté qui s'occupe des rituels. Ils s'occupent de prévoir les choses avant qu'elles ne se produisent et d'être bien préparés. Ce serait un honneur d'être accepté dans les activités d'une telle communauté, tandis que d'autres peuvent la voir différente. Regardez l'âge de la terre et les différentes énergies; influences la plupart des gens prennent en marchant à l'extérieur ou en ouvrant une fenêtre dans la maison. Quand on traite de la sagesse et de la connaissance que l'on peut obtenir de Satan, vous trouverez beaucoup de bonheur, de satisfaction de soi, qui même sous une forme de base est bon parce que l'apprentissage ne s'arrête jamais. La communauté de Satan ne devrait jamais être écartée parce qu'elle offre d'appliquer l'intelligence là où elle doit être. Comprendre l'intelligence est commun pour même un membre du Chemin Satan. (1220)

Chapitre (7): Comment contrôler vos pensées peut Satan vous aider?

Il est important de savoir que nous avons tous la tête pleine de pensées et plus apparaissent dans les moments d'émotions différentes. Pour les gens qui vivent du Chemin Satan, ils sont familiers avec cet événement quotidien à l'intérieur de l'esprit. Ils se sont étudiés au point qu'ils peuvent choisir leurs pensées comme en utilisant leurs mains, au lieu du choix de l'action. Satan joue un rôle majeur dans cette capacité parce qu'elle est encouragée à un moment donné en se joignant au peuple Satan. Ce chapitre aborde la prise de conscience d'un domaine spécifique de sujet, il n'y a aucun désir d'être descriptif. Il faut chercher à se maîtriser dans tous les aspects, surtout en ce qui concerne l'esprit. Il serait préférable d'orienter que d'essayer de simplement comprendre quelque chose de qui ne comprend pas. Satan veut que son peuple ne soit pas victime de ne pas avoir de contrôle de soi ou de pensée.

Chapitre (8): La lettre du Pape satanique (Pape-Jaheem R.Hilts)

Le Darkside a été exquis dans le développement de l'intelligence, depuis sa formulation ancienne. La manière satanique a été discriminée en raison de l'incompréhension de Satan. Les gens louent plutôt les actes malsains sur l'humanité acceptant le tort de certains pairs ou parents et froncent les sourcils sur la croyance religieuse de quelqu'un d'autre. Car l'avenir de La Satanique tout satanique devrait montrer la différence pour diminuer l'ignorance de la perception de la culture satanique. L'avenir du satanique s'épanouira dans le bonheur dans toutes ses affaires. Rappelez-vous les étrangers n'ont pas d'importance si vous faites bien, même en privé. La croissance du satanique sera massive et soigneusement appliquée afin que les gens puissent voir la vérité au lieu de faux dogmes. Ne laissez pas l'ignorance ou le jugement des peuples vous faire remettre en question la réalité quand elle vient de leurs illusions quotidiennes / illusion.

Satanic Pope
(1220) *Jaheem R. Hilts*
May 9th, 2020 11:28pm (MST)

Chapitre (9): Brief about the unseen world

Il était une fois, dans un monde qui ne traitait que des esprits, il y avait une activité constante dans l'utilisation des capacités surnaturelles dans le monde invisible. Tout se passait les esprits cédaient naissance à des esprits; les esprits sont passés par le processus de mourir, même s'ils ne pouvaient pas mourir. Dieu régnait en maître et tout était illuminé par l'esprit royal, Le Créateur de tous en existence. La lumière du Trône était la lumière du monde. Satan était plus bien informé que tous dans le monde spirituel. Il était un maître et il passait du temps à réfléchir aux choses qui existaient. La pensée a traversé l'esprit de Dieu pendant une autre partie de sa création. Satan était plein de joie, il a commencé à jouer de la musique qui a plu à Dieu, Les Anges a même chanté.Then God started manifesting things in existence. Satan pensait que c'était une expansion pour le monde invisible. Satan a vu la gloire et la beauté de Dieu, il a été tenté de parler quand il a vu Dieu former l'homme, puis il a attendu ....

(To be continued)

Biblical Scholar
1220-*Jaheem R.Hilts*

Chapitre (10): Satan doit être compris et non évité

Si nous regardons toute histoire biblique, l'humanité a pris ses propres décisions, de la survie à la capacité. Ils disent "Lucifer a été chassé du ciel" ils disent "Adam et Eve ont été jetés du Jardin d'Eden". Il n'y a personne à blâmer à la fin de la journée. Satan ne devrait pas être évité surtout quand on a la connaissance de Satan, même si l'on ne le fait pas. La raison pour laquelle je dis cela, c'est parce que tout le monde a un choix de libre arbitre. À quoi bon éviter quelqu'un et vous avez le choix de prendre une décision que personne ne peut prendre pour vous. Nous dans L'étreinte satanique Satan parce qu'il est rempli de sagesse que l'homme n'a pas la capacité d'avoir. Nous avons la moindre idée du monde invisible. Satan est une forme différente de création; ceux qui sont initiés peuvent comprendre l'étendue de la façon de communiquer et de comprendre à quoi ils ont affaire. Satan doit être compris et non évité. (1220)

Chapitre (11): L'entrée est importante

Il est important de savoir que l'entrée dans Le Satanique est sensible, très délicate. Il devrait être une question prise très au sérieux et ne pas permettre d'être abusé. C'est un monde à l'intérieur d'un monde, la connaissance ne doit pas être gaspillée. La plupart des gens ne chercheront pas la vérité et la curiosité est commune. L'importance est au-delà de la compréhension des non-initiés. Ceux qui ont des connaissances peuvent vouloir poursuivre la croissance spirituelle; pratiquer la culture de l'unité satanique. Comment on avance avec la capacité de grandir est important, l'amour pour le satanique doit être fort dans une pratique des initiations sur les autres ou l'échec est possible. Comme la lumière brille dans l'obscurité et l'obscurité brille dans la lumière, tout le sera. Ne cherchez jamais à faire l'esprit de quelqu'un d'autre jusqu'à l'abandon / soumission est pour tous les étudiants.

Vertaald naar het Nederlands
Dutch

De meest deskundige zal weten dat Satan er al langer is dan de mensheid. Het misverstand van het individuele begrip van een persoon elimineert verwennerij in hogere erkenning. De geest kan alleen zien in de duisternis, moet men de verboden waarheid worden onderwezen om uit te blinken in een reis die nodig is in alle ogen, vooral het 3e oog. Satan heeft geheimen van Hemel en Aarde geopenbaard aan degenen die hem het meest betrouwbaar zijn; zijn reden om een verklaring af te leggen. Om te geloven in de hulp van Satan, is het gedeeltelijk accepteren dat zelfs Satan is een deel van de hele schepping. Waarom zal men neerkijken op wat ze niet begrijpen? Excuses maken voor hun daden. Satan heeft een rol in dingen die op Aarde plaatsvinden; sommige zijn leuk, sommige als een les. Geef Satan dank voor het sterker maken van je, geef jezelf niet op. (1220)

Hoofdstuk (1): Satan is Oud

Vanaf het begin van de tijd lang voordat bewustzijn zelfs een optie was, bestond Satan. Het universum was vol geesten; andere dingen die alleen in staat waren in de onzichtbare wereld. Intelligentie zou niet eens worden begrepen op een menselijk niveau, omdat de mens niet bestond, behalve in een toekomstig plan. De activiteiten in deze spirituele gebieden zijn nooit in staat geweest tot documentatie. Satan was vóór de creativiteit en de structurele ontwikkeling van architecturale ontwerpen door afgelopen generaties van mensheid. Satan is oud omdat we zijn bestaanstijd niet kunnen berekenen, toen hij geboren of gevormd werd. We zullen weten dat degenen in bijbelse tijden zich bij Satan hebben aangesloten voor wijsheid en het vermogen om verder te kijken dan anderen. Satan is geen dwaas we hebben allemaal keuzes Satan's keuze was prachtig in zijn ogen. Goed en kwaad zijn slechts door degenen waarneming, zondigen heeft geluk gebracht om talloze hoeveelheden mensen per dag, dan langer erkend. Satan hoeft niet voor je te denken, je bent een deel van het begin, ongeacht hoeveel tijd er voorbij gaat.

Hoofdstuk (2): Hoe satan te helpen

Je moet je realiseren dat je Satan helpt. Satan zal willen dat je alle geneugten en verlangens hebt die je voor jezelf wilt. Door Satan te helpen zullen jullie alle zonden in de wereld goedmaken. Je helpt Satan door anderen te helpen; mensen komen samen en genieten van tijd met elkaar op Satan manieren, terwijl zonder is mooi, moet je verspreiden zijn schoonheid. Satan helpen moet niet als een zwakte worden beschouwd, ook al zullen mensen het werk fronsen. Je Satan helpen door niet dom te zijn, door het goede voorbeeld te geven, meer vrede te creëren dan degenen die beweren Goddelijk te zijn. Je Satan helpen door loyaal en betrouwbaar te zijn voor het Satanleger. Er is een strijd tussen goed en kwaad en Satan wil niet alleen bekend staan om het kwaad; Vernietiging.

Hoofdstuk (3): Bekering tot Satan

Ik zou iemand niet aanraden om satan zelf te proberen te begrijpen. Het zou groter zijn om kennis te maken met de Duistere Krachten. Men kan de hoop verliezen om satan te bereiken zonder initiatie. Het vermogen om je te bekeren is net als al het andere, je moet vertrouwen hebben. Geloof in Satan is misschien niet voor iedereen gemakkelijk vanwege de negatieve roddels, opnames van valse interpretaties. Geest, lichaam en ziel moeten erin zitten om voltooiing te ontvangen; niets is heel ontbreekt belangrijk. Bekering tot Satan is gevoelig omdat het in ieder geval geheimzinnig is over het eerste proces, het is zeer gunstig voor degenen die voorbestemd zijn om zich om te zetten uit hun verleden verwarringen. Ik zou andere boeken kunnen verwijzen om het begrip van dit onderwerp te verbreden. Ik kies ervoor om dat niet te doen omdat ze je niet zullen ondersteunen bij het converteren. Satan staat voor verboden kennis of geheime kennis. Bekering tot Satan moet je beginnen met de ontwikkeling, na het dragen van de zaden. Ze zullen groeien, zelfs als je jezelf verzet. Bekering tot Satan is een nieuw begin, een ...

Hoofdstuk (4): Relaties & Satan

Ware liefde is gemakkelijk te vinden in twee mensen die samen willen zijn, gebaseerd op vertrouwen. Het is niet iets gemaakt uit een onbewuste beslissing zowel zal moeten willen hetzelfde. De verboden kennis die wordt doorgegeven aan de ingewijde is voldoende in het omgaan met een relatie situatie. Er is een verbinding die niet kan worden beschreven de wereld wordt gevisualiseerd als aangenamer. Er is geen onzekerheid die kan doordringen, niets onbekends dat jullie een deel kan breken, verwijzend naar (Dark Forces Energy). Satan is geweldig in het houden van zijn volk in geweldige relaties, zowel reizen het pad van Satan. Satan kan ook worden opgemerkt in het maken van goede relaties, wanneer een van zijn volgelingen is, in een relatie met iemand van een ander geloof. Zoals eerder gezegd is Satan oud, dus er is geen theorie dat Satan weet over liefde. Er is geen twijfel dat degenen op het Satanpad liefde met elkaar zullen hebben, dit is natuurlijk als ze het willen. Een relatie opgericht met initiatie, is een gezegende wilde brand containe ...

Hoofdstuk (5): Wijze poëzie van Satan

Als je maar niet verkeerd begrepen werd, hoe helder zal de gloed uit de lucht zijn? Als de formulering van water in de ogen van mijn blote oog leidt mijn geest naar de oudheid, je verschijnt in glorie. De wereld is een weerspiegeling van je bestaan. De gedachten zijn gevuld met onopvallende genoegens. Ik zie je schoonheid, ik wil je gezelschap, en ik weet dat ik niet naïef moet zijn. Door de wolken, als ze me op hen kunnen houden staan. Ik zal de afstand afleggen; Ik zal voor anker gaan en niets anders bezetten dan oneindig.

1220 (Poëzie)

Hoofdstuk (6): Gemeenschap van Satan

Door de eeuwen heen zijn er gemeenschappen geweest die door Satan werden gedreven. Alleen maar omdat een persoon ervoor kiest om de verboden kennis en wijsheid van Satan te volgen, maakt ze niet minder dan wie dan ook die planeet aarde deelt. Een gemeenschap van Satan is een gemeenschap die zich bezighoudt met rituelen. Ze gaan om met het voorzien van dingen voordat ze gebeuren en goed voorbereid. Het zou een eer zijn om zelfs te worden geaccepteerd in de activiteiten van een dergelijke gemeenschap, terwijl anderen het anders kunnen zien. Kijk eens hoe oud de aarde is en de verschillende energieën; invloeden de meeste mensen nemen in gewoon lopen buiten of het openen van een raam in het huis. Wanneer je omgaat met de wijsheid en kennis die je van Satan krijgen, zul je veel geluk, zelfbevrediging vinden, wat zelfs in een basisvorm goed is omdat leren nooit stopt. De gemeenschap van Satan mag nooit worden weggegooid omdat ze aanbieden om intelligentie toe te passen waar het moet zijn. Het begrijpen van intelligentie is gebruikelijk voor zelfs een lid van het Satanpad.

(1220)

Hoofdstuk (7): Hoe je je gedachten beheersen kan Satan je helpen?

Het is belangrijk om te weten dat we een hoofd vol gedachten en meer verschijnen in tijden van verschillende emoties. Voor de mensen die van het Satanpad leven, zijn ze bekend met deze dagelijkse gebeurtenis in de geest. Ze hebben zichzelf bestudeerd tot het punt dat ze hun gedachten kunnen kiezen, zoals het gebruik van hun handen, in plaats van de keuze van de actie. Satan speelt een belangrijke rol in dit vermogen omdat het op een gegeven moment wordt aangemoedigd wanneer hij zich aansluit bij het Satansvolk. Dit hoofdstuk raakt aan het bewustzijn van een specifiek onderwerp is er geen verlangen om te beschrijvend. Men moet proberen om zichzelf te beheersen in alle aspecten vooral omgaan met de geest. Begeleiding zou beter zijn dan proberen om gewoon iets te begrijpen niet begrijpelijk. Satan wil dat zijn volk geen slachtoffer wordt van het niet hebben van zelfbeheersing of gedachtecontrole.

Hoofdstuk (8): De brief van De Satanische Paus (Paus-Jaheem R.Hilts)

De Darkside is voortreffelijk in de ontwikkeling van intelligentie, sinds zijn oude formulering. De Satanische manier is gediscrimineerd vanwege het misverstand van Satan. Mensen prijzen liever ongezonde daden op de mensheid accepteren verkeerd van bepaalde collega's of familieleden en fronsop religieuze overtuiging van iemand anders. Voor de toekomst van Satanic zou alle Satanic het verschil moeten tonen om de onwetendheid van waarneming van de Satanic cultuur te verminderen. De toekomst van satanisch zal bloeien in geluk in al zijn zaken. Herinner jezelf buitenstaanders niet uit als je goed doet, zelfs in prive. De groei van het Satanische zal enorm zijn en zorgvuldig worden toegepast, zodat mensen de waarheid kunnen zien in plaats van valse dogma's. Sta niet toe dat volkeren onwetendheid of oordeel om je vraag werkelijkheid toen het kwam uit hun dagelijkse illusies / waanvoorstellingen.

Satanic Pope
(1220) *Jaheem R.Hilts*
May 9th, 2020 11:28pm (MST)

Hoofdstuk (9): Kort over de onzichtbare wereld

Er was eens, in een wereld die alleen met geesten te maken had, een constante activiteit in het gebruik van bovennatuurlijke vermogens in de onzichtbare wereld. Alles gebeurde geesten waren de geboorte van geesten; geesten gingen door het proces van sterven, ook al konden ze niet sterven. God regeerde oppermachtig en alles werd verlicht door de koninklijke geest, de Schepper van allen in het bestaan. Het licht van De Troon was het licht van de wereld. Satan was meer dan allemaal deskundig in de spirituele wereld. Hij was een meester en hij besteedde tijd aan het nadenken over de dingen in het bestaan. De gedachte kwam bij God op het hoofd voor een ander deel van zijn schepping. Satan was vol vreugde, hij begon muziek te spelen die God beviel, de Engelen zongen zelfs. Toen begon God dingen in het bestaan te manifesteren. Satan dacht dat het een uitbreiding was voor de onzichtbare wereld. Satan zag Gods heerlijkheid en schoonheid, hij was geneigd om te spreken toen hij God de mens zag vormen, toen wachtte hij........

(To be continued)

Biblical Scholar
1220-*Jaheem R. Hilts*

Hoofdstuk (10): Satan moet worden begrepen en niet gemeden

Als we kijken naar alle bijbelse geschiedenis heeft de mensheid zijn eigen beslissingen genomen van overleven tot vermogen. Ze zeggen: "Lucifer werd uit de hemel geworpen" ze zeggen: "Adam en Eva werden gegoten uit de Hof van Eden". Er is niemand de schuld aan het eind van de dag. Satan moet niet worden gemeden wanneer men vooral kennis van Satan heeft, zelfs als men dat niet doet. De reden dat ik dit zeg is omdat iedereen een vrije wil keuze heeft. Wat zou het goed zijn om iemand te mijden en je hebt de keuze om een beslissing niemand kan maken voor je te maken. Wij in het Satanische omarmen Satan omdat hij vervuld is van wijsheid die de mens niet kan hebben. We hebben het minste inzicht in de volledige onzichtbare wereld. Satan is een andere vorm van schepping; De ingewijden kunnen de breedheid begrijpen van hoe te communiceren en te begrijpen waar ze mee te maken hebben. Satan moet begrepen worden en niet gemeden worden. (1220)

Hoofdstuk (11): De ingang is belangrijk

Het is belangrijk om te weten dat de ingang in het Satanisch gevoelig is, zeer delicaat. Het moet een zaak worden die zeer serieus wordt genomen en niet mag worden misbruikt. Het is een wereld in een wereld, kennis mag niet verspild worden. De meeste mensen zullen niet zoeken naar de waarheid en nieuwsgierigheid is gemeenschappelijk. Het belang is onbegrijpelijk voor niet-ingewijden. Degenen met kennis willen misschien de geestelijke groei bevorderen; de cultuur van de Satanische eenheid te beoefenen. Hoe men naar voren komt met het vermogen om te groeien is belangrijk, de liefde voor de Satanische moet sterk zijn in een praktiserende inwijdingen op anderen of falen is mogelijk. Als het licht schijnt in duisternis en duisternis schijnt in het licht, zal het allemaal zijn. Nooit proberen om iemand anders geest overgave / onderwerping is voor alle studenten.

हिंदी में अनुवादित
Hindi

सबसे ज्ञानी को पता होगा कि शैतान मानवजाति की तुलना में लगभग लंबा रहा है। व्यक्ति की व्यक्तिगत समझ से गलतफहमी भोग को उच्च पावती में समाप्त करती है। आत्मा केवल अंधेरे में देख सकते हैं, एक निषिद्ध सत्य सिखाया जाना चाहिए एक सभी आंखों में आवश्यक यात्रा में उत्कृष्टता विशेष रूप से 3 आंख । शैतान ने स्वर्ग और पृथ्वी के रहस्यों को उसके लिए सबसे भरोसेमंद बताया है; उसका कारण बयान देने के लिए । शैतान की मदद में विश्वास करने के लिए, यह आंशिक रूप से स्वीकार कर रहा है कि शैतान भी पूरी सृष्टि का एक हिस्सा है। कोई इस बात पर क्यों

गौर करेगा कि उन्हें क्या समझ में नहीं आता? उनके कार्यों के लिए बहाना बनाना। पृथ्वी पर हो रही चीजों में शैतान की भूमिका होती है; कुछ सुखद हैं, कुछ एक सबक के रूप में । आपको मजबूत बनाने के लिए शैतान को धन्यवाद दें, खुद को न दें। (1220)

अध्याय (1): शैतान प्राचीन है

समय की शुरुआत से लंबे समय से पहले चेतना भी एक विकल्प था, शैतान अस्तित्व में था। ब्रह्मांड सिर्फ आत्माओं से भरा था; अन्य चीजें जो केवल अनदेखी दुनिया में सक्षम थीं। खुफिया भी एक मानव स्तर पर समझ में नहीं आ जाएगा क्योंकि मनुष्य मौजूद नहीं था, एक भविष्य की योजना को छोड़कर । इन आध्यात्मिक स्थानों में गतिविधियों के दस्तावेज में सक्षम नहीं किया गया है। शैतान मानव जाति की पिछली पीढ़ियों द्वारा वास्तुशिल्प डिजाइनों की रचनात्मकता और संरचनात्मक विकास से पहले था। शैतान प्राचीन है क्योंकि हम

अस्तित्व में अपने समय की गणना नहीं कर सकते, जब वह पैदा हुआ था या गठन किया । हम जानते हैं कि बाइबिल के समय में उन लोगों को ज्ञान और दूसरों की तुलना में आगे देखने की क्षमता के लिए शैतान में शामिल हो गए। शैतान कोई मूर्ख नहीं है हम सब विकल्प शैतान की पसंद उसकी आंखों में शानदार था। सही और गलत केवल लोगों की धारणा से कर रहे हैं, पाप दैनिक लोगों की अनगिनत मात्रा में खुशी लाया है, अब से मांयता प्राप्त है । शैतान को आपके लिए सोचने की नहीं है, आप शुरुआत का हिस्सा हैं, चाहे कितना भी समय बीत जाए।

अध्याय (2): शैतान की मदद कैसे करें

आपको यह महसूस करना होगा कि आप शैतान की मदद कर रहे हैं जो आपकी मदद कर रहा है। शैतान चाहता है कि आप सभी सुख और इच्छाओं को आप अपने लिए चाहते हैं। शैतान की मदद करके आप दुनिया के सभी पापों का भला करेंगे। आप दूसरों की मदद करके शैतान की मदद करते हैं; लोग एक साथ आते हैं और शैतान के तरीकों में एक दूसरे के साथ समय का आनंद लेते हैं, जबकि बिना सुंदर है, आपको इसकी सुंदरता फैलानी चाहिए। शैतान की मदद करना एक कमजोरी नहीं माना जाना चाहिए, भले ही लोग काम पर सिकोड़

जाएंगे। आप उदाहरण के द्वारा अग्रणी मूर्ख नहीं होने से शैतान की मदद कर सकते हैं, ईश्वरीय होने का दावा करने वालों की तुलना में अधिक शांति पैदा कर सकते हैं। आप शैतान सेना के प्रति वफादार और भरोसेमंद होने से शैतान की मदद कर सकते हैं। अच्छाई और बुराई के बीच एक लड़ाई है और शैतान सिर्फ बुराई के लिए जाना नहीं चाहता है; विनाश।

अध्याय (3): शैतान में परिवर्तित

मैं किसी को सलाह नहीं दूंगा कि वह खुद से शैतान को समझने की कोशिश करे। इसे डार्क फोर्सेज से शुरू किया जाना ज्यादा होगा । कोई भी बिना दीक्षा के शैतान तक पहुंचने की कोशिश कर आशा खो सकता है। बदलने की क्षमता बाकी सब की तरह है, आपको विश्वास रखना होगा। शैतान में विश्वास नकारात्मक गपशप, झूठी व्याख्याओं की रिकॉर्डिंग के कारण हर किसी के लिए आसान नहीं हो सकता है। मन, शरीर और आत्मा को पूरा करने के लिए उसमें होना चाहिए; कुछ भी नहीं पूरी तरह से महत्वपूर्ण याद आ रही है । शैतान में परिवर्तित करना संवेदनशील है क्योंकि यह कम से कम प्रारंभिक प्रक्रिया को गुप्त करता है, यह उनके पिछले भ्रम से परिवर्तित करने के लिए किस्मत में लोगों के लिए बेहद फायदेमंद है। मैं इस विषय की समझ को

व्यापक बनाने के लिए अन्य पुस्तकों का उल्लेख कर सकता हूं। मैं नहीं चुनता क्योंकि वे आपको परिवर्तित करने का समर्थन नहीं करेंगे। शैतान निषिद्ध ज्ञान या गुप्त ज्ञान का प्रतिनिधित्व करता है। शैतान में परिवर्तित आप को विकसित करने के लिए शुरू किया है, बीज ले जाने के बाद। अगर आप खुद को रोकते हैं तो भी ये बढ़ेंगे। शैतान में परिवर्तित यह एक नई शुरुआत है, एक ...

अध्याय (4): रिश्ते और शैतान

सच्चा प्यार विश्वास के आधार पर एक साथ रहने के इच्छुक दो लोगों में आसानी से मिल जाता है। यह कुछ भी नहीं है एक बेहोश निर्णय दोनों को एक ही बात चाहते हो जाएगा । निषिद्ध ज्ञान है कि शुरू करने के लिए नीचे पारित कर दिया है एक रिश्ते की स्थिति से निपटने में पर्याप्त है । एक कनेक्शन है कि दुनिया का वर्णन नहीं किया जा सकता है और अधिक सुखद के रूप में कल्पना की है । कोई अनिश्चितता नहीं है जो घुसना कर सकती है, कुछ भी अज्ञात नहीं है जो आपको एक हिस्सा तोड़ सकता है, (डार्क फोर्सेज एनर्जी) का जिक्र करता है। शैतान अपने लोगों को भयानक रिश्तों में रखने में महान है, दोनों शैतान के मार्ग की यात्रा करते हैं। शैतान को अच्छे रिश्ते बनाने में भी नोट किया जा सकता है, जब उसका एक अनुयायी होता है, तो किसी

अलग विश्वास के साथ रिश्ते में। जैसा कि शैतान के प्राचीन होने से पहले कहा गया है तो ऐसा कोई सिद्धांत नहीं है जिसे शैतान प्रेम के बारे में जानता है। कोई सवाल ही नहीं है कि शैतान पथ पर उन एक दूसरे के साथ प्यार होगा, यह निश्चित रूप से है अगर वे यह चाहते हैं। एक दीक्षा के साथ स्थापित संबंध है, एक धन्य जंगली आग निहित है ...

अध्याय (5): शैतान की बुद्धिमान कविता

अगर सिर्फ आपको गलतफहमी नहीं हुई तो आसमान से चमक कितनी चमकीली होगी? जैसे मेरी नग्न आंखों की दृष्टि में पानी का निर्माण प्राचीन काल की ओर मेरे मन की ओर जाता है, आप महिमा में दिखाई देते हैं। दुनिया एक प्रतिबिंब है, अपने अस्तित्व का। विचार अपूर्व सुखों से भरे होते हैं। मैं अपनी सुंदरता देखते हैं, मैं अपनी कंपनी चाहते हैं, और मैं भोली नहीं होना पता है। बादलों के माध्यम से, अगर वे मुझे उन पर खड़े पकड़ कर सकते हैं। मैं दूरी की यात्रा करेंगे; मैं अनंत के अलावा कुछ भी नहीं कब्जा लंगर होगा।

1220 (कविता)

अध्याय (6): शैतान का समुदाय

युगों से ऐसे समुदाय रहे हैं जो शैतान द्वारा संचालित थे। सिर्फ इसलिए कि एक व्यक्ति निषिद्ध ज्ञान और शैतान के ज्ञान का पालन करने के लिए चुनता है उंहें किसी और ग्रह पृथ्वी साझा करने से कम नहीं है। शैतान का एक समुदाय एक समुदाय है जो अनुष्ठानों से संबंधित है। वे होने से पहले चीजों की पूर्वायो के साथ सौदा और अच्छी तरह से तैयार किया जा रहा है। यह एक संमान के लिए भी इस तरह के एक समुदाय की गतिविधियों में स्वीकार किया जाएगा, जबकि दूसरों को यह अलग देख सकते हैं। देखो पृथ्वी कितनी पुरानी है और विभिन्न ऊर्जाओं; प्रभाव ज्यादातर लोगों को सिर्फ बाहर चलने या घर में एक खिड़की खोलने में ले लो। जब ज्ञान और ज्ञान से निपटने के लिए एक शैतान से प्राप्त कर सकते हैं, तो आप को बहुत

खुशी, आत्म संतुष्टि मिलेगी, जो बुनियादी रूप में भी अच्छी है क्योंकि सीखना कभी नहीं रुकता है। शैतान के समुदाय को कभी भी त्यागा नहीं जाना चाहिए क्योंकि वे खुफिया जानकारी लागू करने की पेशकश करते हैं जहां इसे होना चाहिए। शैतान पथ के एक सदस्य के लिए खुफिया जानकारी को समझना आम बात है।

(1220)

अध्याय (7): अपने विचारों को कैसे नियंत्रित करें शैतान आपकी मदद कर सकता है?

यह जानना महत्वपूर्ण है कि हमारे पास विचारों से भरा सिर है और विभिन्न भावनाओं के समय में अधिक दिखाई देते हैं। शैतान पथ से दूर रहने वाले लोगों के लिए, वे मन के अंदर इस दैनिक घटना से परिचित हैं। वे खुद को बात वे अपने हाथों का उपयोग कर की तरह अपने विचारों को चुन सकते हैं, बजाय कार्रवाई की पसंद के लिए अध्ययन किया है । शैतान इस क्षमता में एक प्रमुख भूमिका निभाता है क्योंकि यह शैतान लोगों में शामिल होने के दौरान कुछ बिंदु पर प्रोत्साहित किया जाता है। यह अध्याय विषय के एक विशिष्ट क्षेत्र के बारे में जागरूकता को छू रहा है वर्णनात्मक होने की कोई इच्छा नहीं है । एक विशेष रूप से मन से निपटने के सभी पहलुओं में खुद को गुरु की तलाश करनी

चाहिए । मार्गदर्शन बस समझ में नहीं आता कुछ समझने की कोशिश कर से बेहतर होगा । शैतान चाहता है कि उसके लोग आत्म नियंत्रण या विचार नियंत्रण न रखने के शिकार न हों।

अध्याय (8): शैतानी पोप से पत्र (पोप-Jaheem आर Hilts)

डार्कसाइड अपने प्राचीन निर्माण के बाद से, खुफिया के विकास में उत्तम रहा है । शैतान की गलतफहमी के कारण शैतानी तरीके से भेदभाव किया गया है। लोग ⊙ के बजाय मानवता पर अस्वस्थ कृत्यों की प्रशंसा कुछ साथियों या रिश्तेदारों से गलत स्वीकार करने और किसी और के धार्मिक विश्वास पर सिकोड़ी । शैतानी के भविष्य के लिए सभी शैतानी को शैतानी संस्कृति की धारणा की अज्ञानता को कम करने के लिए अंतर दिखाना चाहिए। शैतानी का भविष्य अपने सभी मामलों में खुशी में फलेगा-फूलेगा। अपने आप को याद दिलाएं बाहरी लोगों को कोई फर्क नहीं पड़ता अगर आप सही कर रहे हैं, यहां तक कि निजी में । शैतानी का विकास बड़े पैमाने पर और सावधानी से लागू किया

जाएगा ताकि लोग झूठी हठधर्मिता के बजाय सच्चाई देख सकें। लोगों को अज्ञानता या निर्णय की अनुमति नहीं है आप वास्तविकता सवाल जब यह उनके दैनिक भ्रम से आया/

Satanic Pope
(1220) *Jaheem R.Hilts*
May 9th, 2020 11:28pm (MST)

अध्याय (9): अनदेखी दुनिया के बारे में संक्षिप्त

एक बार एक समय पर, एक दुनिया में केवल आत्माओं से निपटने, वहां अनदेखी दुनिया में अलौकिक क्षमताओं का उपयोग करने में एक निरंतर गतिविधि थी । सब कुछ हो रहा था आत्माओं आत्माओं को जंम दे रहे थे; आत्माओं को मरने की प्रक्रिया के माध्यम से चला गया, भले ही वे मर नहीं सकता है । परमेश्वर ने सर्वोच्च राज किया और सब कुछ शाही आत्मा, अस्तित्व में सभी के निर्माता से प्रकाशित हुआ। सिंहासन से प्रकाश दुनिया की रोशनी थी। शैतान आध्यात्मिक दुनिया में सभी से अधिक जानकार था। वह एक मास्टर था और वह समय बिताया अस्तित्व में चीजों पर विचार । सोचा था कि उसकी रचना के दूसरे भाग के लिए भगवान के मन को पार कर गया। शैतान खुशी से भरा हुआ था, वह संगीत है कि भगवान की कृपा खेलने के लिए शुरू

किया, स्वर्गदूतों भी गाया था। तब भगवान अस्तित्व में चीजों को प्रकट करने लगे। शैतान ने सोचा कि यह अनदेखी दुनिया के लिए एक विस्तार था। शैतान ने परमेश्वर की महिमा और सुंदरता देखी, जब उसने परमेश्वर को मनुष्य बनाते देखा तो वह बोलने के लिए लालायित था, फिर वह इंतजार कर रहा था........

(जारी रखा जाना है)

Biblical Scholar
1220-*Jaheem R.Hilts*

अध्याय (10): शैतान को समझा जाना चाहिए और त्याग नहीं करना चाहिए

अगर हम सभी बाइबिल इतिहास को देखो मानव जाति के अस्तित्व से क्षमता के लिए अपने निर्णय किया है । वे कहते है "लूसिफ़ेर स्वर्ग से बाहर डाली गई थी" वे कहते है "एडम और ईव ईडन गार्डन से डाली गई" । दिन के अंत में दोष देने वाला कोई नहीं है । शैतान को त्याग नहीं दिया जाना चाहिए जब विशेष रूप से किसी को शैतान का ज्ञान हो, भले ही कोई ऐसा न हो। कारण है कि मैं कहता हूं यह है क्योंकि हर कोई एक freewill विकल्प है । क्या अच्छा होगा किसी से दूर है और आप एक निर्णय कोई भी आप के लिए कर सकते है बनाने के लिए विकल्प है । हम शैतान को गले लगाते हैं क्योंकि वह ज्ञान से भरा हुआ है कि मनुष्य के पास कोई क्षमता नहीं है। हम पूरी

अनदेखी दुनिया पर थोड़ी सी भी अंतर्दृष्टि है ।
शैतान सृष्टि का एक अलग रूप है; शुरू किए गए
लोग कैसे संवाद करने और समझने की व्यापकता
को समझ सकते हैं कि वे किस के साथ काम कर
रहे हैं। शैतान को समझना चाहिए और त्याग नहीं
करना चाहिए। (1220)

अध्याय (11): प्रवेश द्वार महत्वपूर्ण है

यह जानना महत्वपूर्ण है कि शैतानी में प्रवेश द्वार संवेदनशील, बहुत नाजुक है। यह एक मामला बहुत गंभीरता से लिया जाना चाहिए और दुर्व्यवहार की अनुमति नहीं दी जानी चाहिए। यह एक संसार के अंदर की दुनिया है, ज्ञान व्यर्थ नहीं जाना चाहिए। ज्यादातर लोग सच्चाई की तलाश नहीं करेंगे और जिज्ञासा आम है। इसका महत्व अदीक्षित की समझ से परे है। ज्ञान वाले लोग आध्यात्मिक विकास को और आगे बढ़ाना चाह सकते हैं; शैतानी एकता की संस्कृति का अभ्यास करें। कैसे एक बढ़ने की क्षमता के साथ आगे आता है महत्वपूर्ण है, शैतानी के लिए प्यार एक दूसरों पर दीक्षा का अभ्यास या विफलता संभव है में मजबूत होना चाहिए। जैसे अंधेरे में प्रकाश चमकता है और अंधेरे प्रकाश में चमकता है, यह सब हो जाएगा। कभी किसी और के मन को

आत्मसमर्पण/प्रस्तुत करने के लिए सभी छात्रों के लिए है की तलाश है ।

日本語に翻訳
Japanese

最も知識のある人は、サタンが人類よりも長く続いていることを知るでしょう。人の個々の理解からの誤解は、より高い認知に甘やかすことを排除します。霊は暗闇の中でしか見ることができない、人はすべての目、特に第三の目に必要な旅行に優れる禁じられた真理を教えられなければなりません。サタンは、彼にとって最も信頼できる人々に天と地の秘密を明らかにしました。彼は声明を出す原因を作った。サタンの助けを信じるには、サタンでさえ創造全体の一部であることを部分的に受け入れられます。なぜ彼らが理解していないことを見下すのでしょうか?彼らの行動の言い訳をする。サタンは地上で起こる事柄に役割を持っています。楽しい人もいれば、レッスンとして楽しい人もいます。あなたを強く

してくれたサタンに感謝し、自分自身を
あきらめないでください。(1220)

章(1):サタンは古代

　意識が選択肢になるずっと前の時代の初めから、サタンは存在していました。宇宙は霊に満ちていた。目に見えない世界でしかできない他のもの。人間は将来の計画を除いて存在しなかったので、知性は人間レベルでは理解されませんでした。これらの霊的な領域での活動は、文書化が可能ではありませんでした。サタンは、人類の過去の世代による建築デザインの創造性と構造開発の前にいました。サタンは、彼が生まれたか形成されたとき、私たちは存在する彼の時間を計算することはできませんので、古代です。聖書の時代の人々は、知恵と他の人よりもさらに見る能力のためにサタンに加わったことを知るでしょう。サタンは、

私たち全員がサタンの選択が彼の目に壮大だった選択肢を持っている愚か者ではありません。正しいことと間違っている人は単に知覚によるものであり、罪を犯すことで、長く認識されるよりも、毎日無数の人々に幸せをもたらしました。サタンはあなたのために考える必要はありません、あなたはどんなに時間が経っても、始まりの一部です。

章(2):サタンを助ける方法

　　あなたはサタンがあなたを助けているのを助けていることに気づく必要があります。サタンはあなたが自分のために望むすべての喜びと欲望を持って欲しいと思うでしょう。サタンを助けることによって、あなたは世のすべての罪を善んにするでしょう。あなたは他の人を助けることによってサタンを助けます。人々は一緒に来て、サタンの方法でお互いに時間を楽しみますが、美しい人がいなければ、あなたはその美しさを広めなければなりません。サタンを助けることは、人々が仕事に眉をひそめるにもかかわらず、弱点と見なされるべきではありません。あなたは、愚かな導きになされず、神の言葉であると公言する者よりも多

くの平和を生み出すことによって、サタンを助けることができます。あなたはサタン軍に忠実で信頼できることによってサタンを助けることができます。善と悪の戦いがあり、サタンは悪のために知られたいだけではありません。破壊。

章(3):サタンへの変換

　　　私は自分でサタンを理解しようとする人に助言しません。ダークフォースに導入されるのが大きいでしょう。人は開始せずにサタンに手を差し伸べようとする希望を失う可能性があります。改宗する能力は他の全てと同じように、あなたは信仰を持たなければなりません。サタンへの信仰は、否定的なゴシップ、誤った解釈の録音のために誰にとっても容易ではないかもしれません。心と体と魂は、完成を受けるためにその中になければなりません。何も全体が重要な欠落していません。サタンへの変換は、少なくとも最初のプロセスを秘密主義であるため、過去の混乱から変換する運命にある人にとっては非常に有益であるため、敏感です。このトピックの理解を深めるために他の本を参照することができました。彼らはあなたが変換をサポートしていないので、私はしないことを選択します。サタンは禁じられた知識や秘密の知識を表しています。サタンに変換するあなたは、種子を運んだ後、開発を開始する必要がありま

す。あなたが自分自身に抵抗しても、彼らは成
長します。サタンに変換すると、それは新しい
始まりです.

第4章:関係とサタン

　　真の愛は、信頼に基づいて、一緒にいた
い2人の人々に簡単に見つかります。それは無
意識の決定から行われたものは何も同じことを
望む必要があります。開始に受け継がれる禁じ
られた知識は、関係の状況を処理するのに十分
です。世の中がもっと楽しいものとして可視化
されるのが説明できないつながりがあります。
浸透できる不確実性はなく、(ダークフォース
エネルギー)を参照して、あなたに部品を壊す
ことができる未知のものはありません。サタン
は、サタンの道を旅する両方の素晴らしい関係
に彼の人々を保つために素晴らしいです。サタ
ンはまた、彼の信者の一人が異なる信仰の誰か
との関係にあるときに、良好な関係を作ること
に注意することができます。サタンの前に述べ
たように古代なので、サタンが愛について知っ
ているという理論はありません。サタンの道に
いる人々がお互いに愛を持つことは間違いあり
ませんが、これはもちろん、彼らがそれを望む

ならばです。開始と設立された関係は、祝福された野生の火の封じ込めです.

章(5):サタンの賢明な詩

　　　あなただけが誤解されていなくても、空からの輝きはどのくらい明るくなりますか?私の肉眼を見て水の定式化が私の心を古代に導くように、あなたは栄光の中に現れます。世界はあなたの存在を反映しています。思いは驚くべき喜びで満たされています。私はあなたの美しさを見て、私はあなたの会社が欲しい、と私はナイーブではないことを知っている。雲を通して、彼らは彼らの上に立って私を保持することができれば。私は距離を移動します。私は無限以外は何も占有しません。

1220 (詩)

第6章:サタン共同体

　　時代を経て、サタンによって動かされたコミュニティがありました。人がサタンの禁じられた知識と知恵に従うことを選んだからといって、地球を共有する他の誰よりも少ないです。サタンのコミュニティは、儀式を扱うコミュニティです。彼らは、彼らが起こる前に物事を予見し、十分に準備されることに対処します。そのようなコミュニティの活動に受け入れられることさえ光栄ですが、他の人はそれを異なって見るかもしれません。地球が何歳か、そして異なるエネルギーを見てください。ほとんどの人が外を歩いたり、家の中で窓を開けたりするだけで影響を受けます。サタンから得られる知恵と知識を扱うとき、学習が止まらないので基本的な形でも良い、多くの幸福、自己満足を見つけるでしょう。サタンのコミュニティは、必要な場所にインテリジェンスを適用することを申し出るので、決して捨てるべきではありません。サタン・パスの一人でも知性を理解することは一般的です。(1220)

章 (7): あなたの考えを制御する方法は、サタンはあなたを助けることができますか?

　　　　私たちは思考に満ちた頭を持っており、より異なる感情の時代に現れることを知ることが重要です。サタンの道を離れて暮らす人々にとって、彼らは心の中でこの日常の出来事に精通しています。彼らは、行動の選択ではなく、自分の手を使うような考えを選ぶことができるところまで自分自身を研究してきました。サタンはサタンの人々に加わるときにある時点で奨励されているので、この能力に大きな役割を果たしています。この章では、特定のトピックの領域に対する認識に触れ、説明的になりたいという願望はありません。人は、特に心を扱うあらゆる面で自分自身を習得しようとする必要があります。ガイダンスは、単に理解できないものを単に理解しようとするよりも良いでしょう。サタンは、自制心や思考制御を持たない人々が犠牲者になることを望んでいます。

章(8):悪魔の教皇(教皇ジャヒームR.ヒルツ)からの手紙

　　　　　ダークサイドは、その古代の製剤以来、知性の開発に絶妙でした。悪魔の方法は、サタンの誤解のために差別されています。人々はむしろ、特定の仲間や親戚から間違った行為を受け入れ、他人の宗教的信念に眉をひそめる人類に対する不健康な行為を賞賛します。悪魔の将来のためにすべての悪魔は悪魔文化の認識の無知を減らす違いを示すべきです。悪魔の未来は、そのすべての事で幸福に繁栄しなければなりません。プライベートでも、あなたが正しいことをしているかどうかは、部外者は関係ありません。悪魔の成長は、人々が偽の独言の代わりに真実を見ることができるように、大規模かつ慎重に適用されなければならない。人々の無知や判断は、それが彼らの毎日の幻想/妄想から来たときに現実に疑問を持たないようにしてください。

Satanic Pope
(1220) *Jaheem R. Hilts*
May 9th, 2020 11:28pm (MST)

章 (9): 目に見えない世界について簡単に説明する

　　　昔々、霊だけを扱う世界では、見えない世界で超自然的な能力を使う活動が絶え間なくありました。すべてが霊を生み出していた。霊は死ぬことができないのに死ぬ過程を経た。神は君臨し、すべてが王室の精神、存在するすべての創造主によって照らされました。玉座からの光は世界の光でした。サタンは霊的な世界の中で何よりも知識が豊富でした。彼はマスターであり、彼は存在するものを熟考する時間を費やしました。その思いは、彼の創造の別の部分のために神の心を越えました。サタンは喜びに満ちていた、彼は神を喜ばせる音楽を演奏し始めた、天使たちも歌った。それから神は存在する事柄を現し始めた。サタンは、それが目に見えない世界のための拡大だと思った。サタンは神の栄光と美しさを見て、神が人を形成するのを見て話すように誘惑され、それから彼は待ちました。(継続)

章(10):サタンは理解され、敬遠されるべきではない

　　　すべての聖書の歴史を見れば、人類は生存から能力に彼自身の決定を下しました。「ルシファーは天国から追い出された」と言われ、「アダムとエバはエデンの園から鋳造された」と言います。一日の終わりに責任を負う人はいません。サタンは、たとえそうでないとしても、サタンの知識を持っている場合は特に敬遠されるべきではありません。私がこれを言う理由は、誰もが自由意志の選択を持っているからです。誰かを敬遠することは何が良いだろうし、誰もあなたのために行うことができる決定を下す選択を持っている。悪魔の中の私たちは、人間が持つ能力を持たない知恵で満たされているので、サタンを受け入れます。私たちは、完全な目に見えない世界に関するわずかな洞察を持っています。サタンは創造の形が異なる。開始された人々は、彼らが何を扱っているかを伝え、理解する方法の広さを理解することができま

す。サタンは理解され、敬遠されるべきではあ
りません。(1220)

章(11):入り口は重要

　悪魔への入り口は敏感で、非常に繊細であることを知ることが重要です。それは非常に真剣に取られ、虐待を受けることを許されない問題であるべきです。それは世界の中の世界であり、知識を無駄にしてはならない。ほとんどの人は真実を求めないだろうし、好奇心は一般的です。重要性は初心者の理解を超えています。知識を持つ人々は,さらに霊的な成長を望むかもしれません。悪魔の団結の文化を実践する。成長する能力を持ってどのように前進するかは重要であり、悪魔への愛は他の人に対する練習の開始や失敗に強くなければならない。光が暗闇の中で輝き、暗闇が光の中で輝く中で、それはすべてになります。決して他の人の心を降伏/提出するすべての学生のためのものです。

Aistrithe go Gaeilge
Irish

Beidh a fhios ag an chuid is mó eolach go bhfuil Satan thart níos faide ná an cine daonna. Cuireann an míthuiscint ó thuiscint aonair duine deireadh le hindulgence isteach admháil níos airde. Ní féidir leis an spiorad a fheiceáil ach amháin sa dorchadas, ní mór an fhírinne toirmiscthe a mhúineadh chun barr feabhais a bhaint amach i dtaisteal atá riachtanach i ngach súile go háirithe an 3ú súl. Satan Léirigh rúin na bhFlaitheas agus an Domhain dóibh siúd is iontaofa dó; a chúis ráiteas a dhéanamh. Chun a chreidiúint i gcabhair ar Satan, tá sé ag glacadh go páirteach go bhfuil fiú Satan mar chuid den chruthú ar fad. Cén fáth a bhféachfaidh duine síos ar an méid nach dtuigeann siad? Leithscéalta a dhéanamh as a gcuid gníomhartha. Tá ról ag Satan i rudaí atá ar siúl ar an Domhan; tá cuid acu taitneamhach, cuid acu mar cheacht. Buíochas a ghabháil le Satan as tú a dhéanamh níos láidre, ná tabhair suas duit féin. (1220)

Caibidil (1): Is Satan Ársa

Ó thús an ama i bhfad sula raibh an chonaic fiú rogha, bhí Satan ann. Bhí na cruinne ach lán de bhiotáille; rudaí eile nach raibh in ann ach sa domhan gan choinne. ['Ní bheadh Faisnéis a thuiscint fiú ar leibhéal an duine toisc nach raibh daoine ann, ach amháin i bplean sa todhchaí.\n'] Ní raibh na gníomhaíochtaí sna réimsí spioradálta seo in ann doiciméadú a dhéanamh riamh. Bhí Satan roimh chruthaitheacht agus forbairt struchtúrach dearaí ailtireachta ag na glúnta seo caite den chine daonna. Tá Satan ársa toisc nach féidir linn a chuid ama a ríomh ann, nuair a rugadh nó nuair a bunaíodh é. Beidh a fhios againn siúd in amanna bíobalta chuaigh Satan le haghaidh eagna agus an cumas a fheiceáil níos faide ná a chéile. Níl aon amadán againn go léir go raibh rogha Satan iontach ina shúile. Níl ar dheis agus mícheart ach dearcadh na ndaoine, thug sinning sonas do mhéideanna neamhchinnte daoine go laethúil, níos faide ná mar a aithnítear. Ní gá do Satan smaoineamh ar do shon, tá tú mar chuid den tús, is cuma cé mhéad ama a théann.

Caibidil (2): Conas cabhrú le Satan

Caithfidh tú a thuiscint go bhfuil tú ag cabhrú le Satan tá sé ag cabhrú leat. Beidh Satan ag iarraidh go mbeidh na pléisiúir agus na mianta go léir is mian leat duit féin. Trí chabhrú le Satan déanfaidh tú go maith de gach peacaar ar fud an domhain. Cabhraíonn tú le Satan trí chabhrú le daoine eile; daoine teacht le chéile agus taitneamh a bhaint as am lena chéile ar bhealaí Satan, cé go bhfuil pheaca álainn, ní mór duit a scaipeadh ar a áilleacht. Níor chóir a mheas gur laige é cuidiú le Satan, cé go mbeidh daoine ag frown ar an obair. Is féidir leat cabhrú le Satan trí gan a bheith foolish rá trí shampla, ag cruthú níos mó síochána ná iad siúd a professing a bheith Godly. Is féidir leat cabhrú le Satan trí bheith dílis agus iontaofa don Arm Satan. Tá cath idir maith agus olc agus Ní Satan ag iarraidh ach a bheith ar eolas le haghaidh olc; scrios.

Caibidil (3): Athrú go Satan

Ní mholfainn do dhuine iarracht a dhéanamh Satan a thuiscint leo féin. Bheadh sé níos mó a thabhairt isteach sna Fórsaí Dorcha. Is féidir a chailleadh dóchas ag iarraidh a bhaint amach chun Satan gan tionscnamh. ['Is é an cumas a thiontú cosúil le gach eile, caithfidh tú a bheith creideamh.\n'] ['Ní féidir Creideamh i Satan a bheith éasca do gach duine mar gheall ar an gossip diúltach, taifeadtaí de léirmhínithe bréagach.\n'] Ní mór aigne, comhlacht agus anam a bheith ann chun críochnú a fháil; níl aon rud ar iarraidh rud éigin tábhachtach. Tá athrú go Satan íogair toisc go bhfuil sé rúnda an próiseas tosaigh ar a laghad, tá sé an-tairbheach dóibh siúd atá i ndán a thiontú óna mearbhall roimhe seo. D'fhéadfainn tagairt a dhéanamh do leabhair eile chun tuiscint ar an ábhar seo a leathnú. Roghnaím gan toisc nach dtacóidh siad leat a athrú. Is ionann Satan agus eolas toirmiscthe nó eolas rúnda. Athrú go Satan caithfidh tú tosú ag forbairt, tar éis na síolta a iompar. Fásfaidh siad fiú má chuireann tú in aghaidh tú féin. ['Athrú go Satan tá sé tús nua, a ...\n']

['Caibidil (4): Caidrimh & Satan\n']

Tá grá fíor le fáil go héasca i mbeirt daoine
ar mian leo a bheith le chéile, bunaithe ar
iontaobhas. Ní rud ar bith é a rinneadh as cinneadh
neamhfhiosach beidh ar an dá cheann an rud céanna
a iarraidh. Is leor an t-eolas toirmiscthe a chuirtear ar
aghaidh go dtí an tionscnamh chun staid chaidrimh a
láimhseáil. Tá nasc nach féidir cur síos a dhéanamh
ar an domhan léirshamhlú mar níos taitneamhaí. Níl
aon neamhchinnteacht ann ar féidir leis dul i bhfód,
rud ar bith anaithnid ar féidir leo cuid a bhriseadh,
ag tagairt do (Fuinneamh Fórsaí Dorcha). Tá Satan
iontach chun a mhuintir a choinneáil i gcaidrimh
uamhnach, agus iad araon ag taisteal cosán Satan. Is
féidir satan a thabhairt faoi deara freisin i gcaidrimh
mhaith a dhéanamh, nuair a bhíonn duine dá lucht
leanúna, i gcaidreamh le duine de mheon difriúil.
Mar a luadh roimh Satan ársa mar sin níl aon teoiric
ann a fhios ag Satan faoi ghrá. Níl aon cheist ann go
mbeidh grá ag na daoine sin ar an gcosán Satan lena
chéile, is é seo ar ndóigh más mian leo é. Is é an
caidreamh a bunaíodh le tionscnamh, ina tine fiáin
bheannaigh ...

Caibidil (5): Filíocht chiallmhar Satan

Más rud é nach raibh tú misunderstood ach, cé chomh geal a bheidh an glow as an spéir a bheith? De réir mar a bhíonn m'intinn ag foirmliú uisce i radharc mo shúile naked go hamanna ársa, tá tú le feiceáil i nglóir. Is machnamh é an domhan, ar do bheith ann. Líontar na smaointe le pléisiúir nach bhfuil suntasach. Feicim do áilleacht, ba mhaith liom do chuideachta, agus tá a fhios agam gan a bheith naive. Trí na scamaill, más féidir leo seasamh orm. Taistealóidh mé an t-achar; Beidh mé ancaire áitiú rud ar bith ach amháin gan teorainn.

1220 (Filíocht)

Caibidil (6): Comhphobal Satan

Trí na haoiseanna bhí pobail a bhí á dtiomáint ag Satan. Díreach mar a roghnaíonn duine an t-eolas toirmiscthe agus eagna Satan a leanúint ní dhéanann siad níos lú ná aon duine eile a roinnt domhan phláinéid. Is pobal de Satan pobal a dhéileálann le deasghnátha. Déileálann siad le rudaí a thuar sula dtarlaíonn siad agus a bheith ullmhaithe go maith. ['Bheadh sé ina onóir a ghlacadh fiú i ngníomhaíochtaí den sórt sin pobail, agus d'fhéadfadh daoine eile a fheiceáil sé difriúil.\n'] Féach cé chomh sean is atá an domhan agus na fuinneamh éagsúla; bíonn tionchar ag formhór na ndaoine ar siúl taobh amuigh nó fuinneog a oscailt sa teach. Nuair a bhíonn tú ag déileáil leis an eagna agus an t-eolas is féidir le duine a fháil ó Satan, gheobhaidh tú a lán sonas, féinshástacht, a bhfuil fiú i bhfoirm bhunúsach maith toisc nach stopann foghlaim riamh. Níor chóir pobal Satan a chaitheamh i leataobh riamh toisc go dtugann siad faisnéis a chur i bhfeidhm nuair is gá dó a bheith. Tá faisnéis a thuiscint coitianta do fiú ball amháin den Chonair Satan.

(1220)

Caibidil (7): Conas do chuid smaointe a rialú is féidir le Satan cabhrú leat?

Tá sé tábhachtach go mbeadh a fhios againn go bhfuil ceann iomlán smaointe againn go léir agus go bhfuil níos mó le feiceáil in amanna mothúcháin éagsúla. Maidir leis na daoine a chónaíonn as An Cosán Satan, tá siad eolach ar an tarlú laethúil seo taobh istigh den intinn. Rinne siad staidéar orthu féin go dtí an pointe gur féidir leo a gcuid smaointe a roghnú mar a lámha a úsáid, seachas an rogha gníomhaíochta. Tá ról mór ag Satan sa chumas seo toisc go spreagtar é ag pointe áirithe nuair a théann sé isteach i ndaoine Satan. Tá an chaibidil seo i dteagmháil le feasacht ar réimse sonrach ábhair níl aon mhian le tuairisciú. Ní mór iarracht a dhéanamh iad féin a mháistir i ngach gné go háirithe ag déileáil leis an intinn. Bheadh treoir níos fearr ná iarracht a dhéanamh rud éigin nach bhfuil intuigthe a thuiscint. ['Satan ba mhaith leis a chuid daoine gan a bheith íospartaigh nach bhfuil féin-rialú nó rialú smaoinimh.\n']

Caibidil (8): An litir ón Pápa Satanic (Pápa-Jaheem R.Hilts)

Tá an Darkside fíorálainn i bhforbairt na faisnéise, ó shílliú ársa. Rinneadh idirdhealú ar an mbealach Satanic mar gheall ar mhíthuiscint Satan. Molann daoine gníomhartha míshláintiúla ar an gcine daonna ag glacadh mícheart ó chomhghleacaithe nó ó ghaolta áirithe agus frown ar chreideamh reiligiúnach duine eile. Maidir le todhchaí an Satanic ba chóir go léir Satanic thaispeáint ar an difríocht a laghdú ar an aineolas ar an dearcadh ar an cultúr Satanic. Tiocfaidh borradh faoi thodhchaí an satanatach i sonas ina ghnóthaí go léir. Cuir i gcuimhne duit féin lasmuigh ábhar má tá tú ag déanamh ceart, fiú go príobháideach. Beidh fás an Satanic a chur i bhfeidhm ollmhór agus go cúramach ionas gur féidir le daoine a fheiceáil ar an fhírinne in ionad dogma bréagach. Ná lig do dhaoine aineolas nó breithiúnas a dhéanamh ceist tú réaltacht nuair a tháinig sé as a n-illusions laethúil / delusion.

Satanic Pope

(1220) *Jaheem R.Hilts*

May 9th, 2020 11:28pm (MST)

211

Caibidil (9): Gearr faoin domhan gan choinne

Nuair ar am, i saol amháin ag déileáil le biotáillí, bhí gníomhaíocht leanúnach i úsáid a bhaint as cumais osnádúrtha sa domhan gan choinne. Bhí gach rud ag tarlú biotáillí ag tabhairt breithe do bhiotáille; chuaigh biotáillí tríd an bpróiseas ag fáil bháis cé nach bhféadfadh siad bás a fháil. Dia reigned uachtarach agus bhí soilsithe gach rud ag an spiorad ríoga, An Cruthaitheoir ar fad ann. Ba é solas an Ríchathaoir solas an domhain. Bhí satan eolach níos mó ná gach duine sa domhan spioradálta. Bhí sé ina mháistir agus chaith sé am ag smaoineamh ar na rudaí atá ann. Thrasnaigh an smaoineamh intinn Dé do chuid eile dá chruthú. Bhí Satan lán áthais, thosaigh sé ag imirt ceoil a bhí sásta le Dia, The Angels fiú sang. Ansin thosaigh Dia rudaí a léiriú ann. Shíl Satan go raibh sé ina leathnú don domhan gan choinne. Satan le feiceáil glóir Dé agus áilleacht, bhí sé tempted a labhairt nuair a chonaic sé Dia ag teacht fear, ansin d'fhan sé ....

(Le leanúint ar aghaidh)

Biblical Scholar
1220-*Jaheem R. Hilts*

Caibidil (10): Ba chóir Satan a thuiscint agus gan a bheith shunned

Má fhéachaimid ar gach cine daonna stair biblical rinne a chinntí féin ó mharthanas go cumas. Deir siad "Caitheadh Lucifer as neamh" a deir siad "Caitheadh Adam and Eve ó Ghairdín Eden". Níl aon duine chun an milleán ag deireadh an lae. Níor chóir Satan a shunned go háirithe nuair a bhíonn eolas ag duine ar Satan, fiú mura bhfuil ceann amháin. Is é an chúis a deirim é seo toisc go bhfuil rogha saor in aisce ag gach duine. Cad maith a bheadh sé a shun duine éigin agus tá tú an rogha a dhéanamh cinneadh is féidir aon duine a dhéanamh ar do shon. Táimid sa Satanic glacadh Satan toisc go bhfuil sé líonadh le eagna go bhfuil fear aon chumas a bheith acu. Tá an léargas is lú againn ar an domhan iomlán gan choinne. Is cineál difriúil cruthaithe é Satan; is féidir leo siúd a tionscnaíodh tuiscint a fháil ar an leathant a bhaineann le conas cumarsáid a dhéanamh agus tuiscint a fháil ar an méid atá siad ag déileáil leo. Ba chóir satan a thuiscint agus ní shunned. (1220)

Caibidil (11): Tá an bealach isteach tábhachtach

Tá sé tábhachtach go mbeadh a fhios go bhfuil an bealach isteach sa Satanic íogair, an-íogair. Ba chóir go mbeadh sé ina ábhar a glacadh an-dáiríre agus gan cead a bheith mí-úsáid. Is domhan taobh istigh de domhan é, níor cheart eolas a chur amú. Ní lorgóidh formhór na ndaoine an fhírinne agus tá fiosracht coitianta. Tá an tábhacht thar thuiscint ar an gan tionscnaíodh. B'fhéidir gur mhaith leo siúd a bhfuil eolas acu fás spioradálta breise; cultúr aontacht Satanic a chleachtadh. ['Conas a thagann duine ar aghaidh leis an gcumas chun fás tábhachtach, ní mór an grá do The Satanic a bheith láidir i gceann tionscnaimh cleachtadh ar dhaoine eile nó teip is féidir.\n'] De réir mar a shines solas i dorchadas agus shines dorchadas i bhfianaise, beidh sé go léir. Ná déan iarracht riamh géilleadh/aighneacht duine eile a dhéanamh suas do gach mac léinn.

Tradotto in italiano
Italian

I più esperti sapranno che Satana è stato in giro più a lungo dell'umanità. L'incomprensione dalla comprensione individuale di una persona elimina l'indulgenza in un riconoscimento superiore. Lo spirito può vedere solo nelle tenebre, bisogna insegnare la verità proibita a eccellere in un viaggio necessario a tutti gli occhi, specialmente il terzo occhio. Satana ha rivelato segreti del Cielo e della Terra a i più fidati di lui; la sua causa di fare una dichiarazione. Credere nell'aiuto di Satana, è parzialmente accettare che anche Satana sia parte dell'intera creazione. Perché si guarderà dall'basso ciò che non capiscono? Scusandomi per le loro azioni. Satana ha un ruolo nelle cose che si svolgono sulla Terra; alcuni sono piacevoli, alcuni come una lezione. Ringrazia Satana per averti reso più forte, non arrenderti a te stesso. (1220)

Capitolo (1): Satana è antico

Fin dall'inizio dei tempi molto prima che la coscienza fosse ancora un'opzione, Satana esisteva. L'universo era pieno di spiriti; altre cose che erano capaci solo nel mondo invisibile. L'intelligenza non sarebbe nemmeno compresa a livello umano perché gli esseri umani non esistevano, se non in un piano futuro. Le attività in questi regni spirituali non sono mai state capaci di documentare. Satana era prima della creatività e dello sviluppo strutturale dei disegni architettonici delle generazioni passate dell'umanità. Satana è antico perché non possiamo calcolare il suo tempo di esistenza, quando è nato o formato. Conosceremo coloro che in tempi biblici si sono uniti a Satana per la saggezza e la capacità di vedere più di altri. Satana non è sciocco che tutti noi abbiamo scelte la scelta di Satana è stata magnifica ai suoi occhi. Il bene e il male sono semplicemente per percezione di chi, il peccato ha portato felicità a innumerevoli quantità di persone ogni giorno, più a lungo del riconoscimento. Satana non deve pensare per voi, siete una parte dell'inizio, non importa quanto tempo passa.

Capitolo (2): Come aiutare Satana

Devi capire che stai aiutando Satana che ti`sta aiutando. Satana vorrà che tu abbia tutti i piaceri e i desideri che vuoi per te stesso. Aiutando Satana, farete bene a tutti i peccati del mondo. Voi aiutate Satana aiutando gli altri; le persone si riuniscono e si divertono a divertirsi in modo satana, mentre il peccato è bello, devi diffondere la sua bellezza. Aiutare Satana non deve essere considerato una debolezza, anche se le persone si accigliano sull'opera. Potete aiutare Satana non essendo sciocco guidando con l'esempio, creando più pace di coloro che professano di essere divini. Puoi aiutare Satana essendo leale e affidabile per l'Armata Satana. C'è una battaglia tra il bene e il male e Satana non vuole solo essere conosciuto per il male; Distruzione.

Capitolo (3): Conversione a Satana

Non consiglierei a qualcuno di cercare di capire Satana da solo. Sarebbe più grande essere introdotti nelle Forze Oscure. Si può perdere la speranza cercando di raggiungere Satana senza intuire. La capacità di convertirsi è come ogni altra cosa, devi avere fede. La fede in Satana potrebbe non essere facile per tutti a causa dei pettegolezzi negativi, registrazioni di false interpretazioni. La mente, il corpo e l'anima devono essere in essa per ricevere il completamento; nulla manca a qualcosa di importante. Convertirsi a Satana è sensibile perché almeno il processo segreto è segreto, è molto vantaggioso per coloro che sono destinati a convertire dalle loro confusioni passate. Potrei fare riferimento ad altri libri per ampliare la comprensione di questo argomento. Ho scelto di non farlo perché non ti sosterranno la conversione. Satana rappresenta la conoscenza proibita o la conoscenza segreta. Conversione a Satana devi iniziare a sviluppare, dopo aver portato i semi. Cresceranno anche se resisterai a te stesso. La conversione a Satana è un nuovo inizio, un ...

Capitolo (4): Relazioni e Satana

Il vero amore si trova facilmente in due persone che vogliono stare insieme, sulla base della fiducia. Non è niente preso da una decisione inconscia che entrambi dovranno volere la stessa cosa. La conoscenza proibita che viene tramandata all'iniziato è sufficiente nella gestione di una situazione di relazione. C'è una connessione che non può essere descritta il mondo è visualizzato come più piacevole. Non c'è incertezza che possa penetrare, niente di sconosciuto che possa spezzarti una parte, riferendosi a (Energia forze oscure). Satana è grande nel mantenere il suo popolo in relazioni impressionanti, entrambi percorrono il cammino di Satana. Satana può anche essere notato nel fare buoni rapporti, quando uno dei suoi seguaci è, in un rapporto con qualcuno di una fede diversa. Come detto prima di Satana è antico, quindi non c'è teoria che Satana conosca l'amore. Non c'è dubbio che coloro che si trovano sul sentiero di Satana avranno amore con l'altro, questo ovviamente è se lo vogliono. Un rapporto fondato con l'avvio, è un benedetto fuoco selvaggio contenere ...

Capitolo (5): Saggia poesia di Satana

Se solo non foste stati fraintesi, quanto sarà luminoso il bagliore dal cielo? Mentre la formulazione dell'acqua alla vista del mio occhio nudo porta la mia mente ai tempi antichi, tu appari in gloria. Il mondo è un riflesso, della vostra esistenza. I pensieri sono pieni di piaceri insignificanti. Vedo la tua bellezza, voglio la tua compagnia, e so che non essere ingenua. Attraverso le nuvole, se mi tengono in piedi su di loro. Percorrerò la distanza; Ancoraggio occupando nulla se non infinito.

1220 (Poesia)

Capitolo (6): Comunità di Satana

Nel corso dei secoli ci sono state comunità che sono state guidate da Satana. Solo perché una persona sceglie di seguire la conoscenza proibita e la saggezza di Satana non le rende meno di chiunque altro che condivide il pianeta terra. Una comunità di Satana è una comunità che si occupa di rituali. Si occupano di prevedere le cose prima che accadano ed essere ben preparati. Sarebbe un onore anche essere accettati nelle attività di una tale comunità, mentre altri possono vederla diversa. Guardate quanti anni ha la terra e le diverse energie; influenza la maggior parte delle persone prendono solo a piedi fuori o l'apertura di una finestra in casa. Quando si ha a che fare con la saggezza e la conoscenza che si può ottenere da Satana, troverete molta felicità, autosoddisfazione, che anche in una forma di base è buona perché l'apprendimento non si ferma mai. La comunità di Satana non dovrebbe mai essere scartata perché si offre di applicare l'intelligenza dove deve essere. Comprendere l'intelligenza è comune anche per un membro del Sentiero di Satana.

(1220)

Capitolo (7): Come controllare i vostri pensieri Satana può aiutarvi?

È importante sapere che tutti noi abbiamo una testa piena di pensieri e più appaiono in tempi di emozioni diverse. Per le persone che vivono del Sentiero satana, hanno familiarità con questo avvenimento quotidiano all'interno della mente. Hanno studiato se stessi al punto che possono scegliere i loro pensieri come usare le mani, invece della scelta dell'azione. Satana gioca un ruolo importante in questa abilità perché è incoraggiato ad un certo punto quando si unisce al popolo Satana. Questo capitolo tocca la consapevolezza di un'area specifica dell'argomento non c'è alcun desiderio di essere descrittivi. Bisogna cercare di padroneggiare se stessi in tutti gli aspetti, in particolare trattare con la mente. L'orientamento sarebbe meglio che cercare di capire semplicemente qualcosa di non comprensibile. Satana vuole che il suo popolo non sia vittima di non avere autocontrollo o controllo del pensiero.

Capitolo (8) La lettera del Papa satanico (Papa-Jaheem R.Hilts)

Il Darkside è stato squisito nello sviluppo dell'intelligenza, fin dalla sua antica formulazione. Il modo satanico è stato discriminato a causa dell'incomprensione di Satana. Le persone preferiscono lodare gli atti malsani quando l'umanità accetta male da certi coetanei o parenti e si acciglia sul credo religioso di qualcun altro. Per il futuro di The Satanic tutto satanico dovrebbe mostrare la differenza per diminuire l'ignoranza della percezione della cultura satanica. Il futuro di The Satanic fiorirà nella felicità in tutti i suoi affari. Ricordaa a te stesso gli estranei non importa se stai facendo bene, anche in privato. La crescita di The Satanic sarà massiccia e applicata con cura in modo che le persone possano vedere la verità invece di falsi dogmi. Non permettere ai popoli di ignorare o giudicare per farti mettere in discussione la realtà quando è venuta dalle loro illusioni quotidiane / illusione.

Satanic Pope

(1220) *Jaheem R.Hilts*

May 9th, 2020 11:28pm (MST)

Capitolo (9): Breve sul mondo invisibile

C'era una volta, in un mondo che ha a che fare solo con gli spiriti, c'era una costante attività nell'usare abilità soprannaturali nel mondo invisibile. Tutto stava accadendo spiriti stavano dando vita a spiriti; spiriti ha attraversato il processo di morte, anche se non potevano morire. Dio regnò supremo e tutto era illuminato dallo spirito reale, il Creatore di tutti gli esistenti. La luce del Trono era la luce del mondo. Satana era ben informato più di tutti nel mondo spirituale. Era un maestro e passava del tempo a meditare sulle cose esistenti. Il pensiero attraversò la mente di Dio per un'altra parte della sua creazione. Satana era pieno di gioia, cominciò a suonare la musica che piaceva a Dio, gli Angeli cantavano anche. Allora Dio cominciò a manifestare le cose esistenti. Satana pensò che fosse un'espansione per il mondo invisibile. Satana vide la gloria e la bellezza di Dio, fu tentato di parlare quando vide Dio formare l'uomo, poi attese .... (Per continuare)

Biblical Scholar
1220-*Jaheem R.Hilts*

226

Capitolo (10): Satana deve essere compreso e non evitato

Se guardiamo a tutta la storia biblica l'umanità ha preso le proprie decisioni dalla sopravvivenza alla capacità. Dicono che "Lucifero è stato cacciato dal cielo" dicono "Adamo ed Eva sono stati cacciati dal Giardino dell'Eden". Non c'è nessuno da incolpare alla fine della giornata. Satana non dovrebbe essere evitato, specialmente quando si ha la conoscenza di Satana, anche se non si ha conoscenza di Satana, anche se non si è. La ragione per cui dico questo è perché tutti hanno una libera scelta. A che serve evitare qualcuno e che tu abbia la possibilità di prendere una decisione che nessuno può prendere per te. Noi in The Satanic abbracciano Satana perché egli è pieno di saggezza che l'uomo non ha la capacità di avere. Abbiamo la minima intuizione su tutto il mondo invisibile. Satana è una forma diversa di creazione; gli iniziati possono comprendere l'ampiezza di come comunicare e capire con cosa hanno a che fare. Satana dovrebbe essere compreso e non evitato. (1220)

Capitolo (11): L'ingresso è importante

È importante sapere che l'ingresso nel Satanico è sensibile, molto delicato. Dovrebbe trattarsi di una questione presa molto sul serio e non consentita di essere abusata. È un mondo all'interno di un mondo, la conoscenza non deve essere sprecata. La maggior parte delle persone non cercherà la verità e la curiosità è comune. L'importanza è al di là della comprensione dei non iniziati. Coloro che hanno conoscenze potrebbero voler promuovere la crescita spirituale; pratica la cultura dell'unità satanica. Il modo in cui si fa avanti la capacità di crescere è importante, l'amore per il satanico deve essere forte in una pratica sulle altre o il fallimento è possibile. Mentre la luce risplende nell'oscurità e l'oscurità risplende di luce, tutto sarà. Non cercare mai di rendere la mente di qualcun altro up arrendersi / sottomissione è per tutti gli studenti.

Traduzido para o português
Portuguese

229

Os mais experientes saberão que Satanás existe há mais tempo que a humanidade. O equívoco da compreensão individual de uma pessoa elimina a indulgência em maior reconhecimento. O espírito só pode ver na escuridão, deve-se ensinar a verdade proibida para se sobressair em uma viagem necessária em todos os olhos, especialmente no terceiro olho. Satanás revelou segredos do Céu e da Terra para aqueles mais confiáveis para ele; sua causa para fazer uma declaração. Acreditar na ajuda de Satanás, é parcialmente aceito que até Satanás faz parte de toda a criação. Por que alguém vai olhar para baixo sobre o que eles não entendem? Inventando desculpas para suas ações. Satanás tem um papel nas coisas que acontecem na Terra; alguns são agradáveis, outros como lição. Agradeça a Satanás por te fazer mais forte, não desista de si mesmo. (1220)

Capítulo (1): Satanás é antigo

Desde o início dos tempos, muito antes da consciência ser uma opção, Satanás existia. O universo estava cheio de espíritos; outras coisas que só eram capazes no mundo invisível. A inteligência nem seria entendida em um nível humano porque os humanos não existiam, exceto em um plano futuro. As atividades nesses reinos espirituais nunca foram capazes de documentação. Satanás estava diante da criatividade e desenvolvimento estrutural dos projetos arquitetônicos pelas gerações passadas da humanidade. Satanás é antigo porque não podemos calcular seu tempo de existência, quando ele nasceu ou se formou. Saberemos que aqueles em tempos bíblicos se juntaram a Satanás para a sabedoria e a capacidade de ver mais longe do que os outros. Satanás não é tolo, todos temos escolhas A escolha de Satanás foi magnífica aos olhos dele. O certo e o errado são meramente pela percepção dos entes, o pecado trouxe felicidade a inúmeras quantidades de pessoas diariamente, mais do que reconhecidas. Satanás não tem que pensar para você, você é uma parte do começo, não importa ho ...

Capítulo (2): Como ajudar Satanás

Você tem que perceber que ajudar Satanás está te ajudando. Satanás vai querer que você tenha todos os prazeres e desejos que você quer para si mesmo. Ajudando Satanás, você fará o bem de todos os pecados do mundo. Você ajuda Satanás ajudando os outros; as pessoas se reúnem e aproveitam o tempo umas com as outras em satanás, enquanto o pecado é bonito, você deve espalhar sua beleza. Ajudar Satanás não deve ser considerado uma fraqueza, mesmo que as pessoas desaleirem o trabalho. Você pode ajudar Satanás não sendo tolo liderando pelo exemplo, criando mais paz do que aqueles que professam ser piedosos. Você pode ajudar Satanás sendo leal e confiável para o Exército de Satanás. Há uma batalha entre o bem e o mal e

Satanás não quer apenas ser conhecido pelo mal; Destruição.

Capítulo (3): Conversão para Satanás

Eu não aconselharia alguém a tentar entender Satanás sozinho. Seria maior ser apresentado às Forças das Trevas. Pode-se perder a esperança tentando chegar a Satanás sem iniciação. A habilidade de se converter é como tudo, você tem que ter fé. A fé em Satanás pode não ser fácil para todos por causa das fofocas negativas, gravações de falsas interpretações. Mente, corpo e alma têm que estar nele para receber a conclusão; nada está faltando algo importante. Converter-se para Satanás é sensível porque é secreto o processo inicial, pelo menos, é altamente benéfico para aqueles destinados a se converter de suas confusões passadas. Eu poderia referenciar outros livros para ampliar a compreensão deste tema. Eu escolho não fazer isso porque eles não vão apoiá-lo se convertendo. Satanás representa conhecimento proibido ou conhecimento secreto. Convertendo-se para Satanás você tem que começar a desenvolver, depois de carregar as sementes. Eles crescerão mesmo se você resistir a si mesmo. Converter para Satanás é um novo começo, um...

Capítulo (4): Relacionamentos & Satanás

O amor verdadeiro é facilmente encontrado em duas pessoas querendo ficar juntas, baseadas na confiança. Não é nada feito de uma decisão inconsciente ambos terão que querer a mesma coisa. O conhecimento proibido que é passado para o iniciado é suficiente para lidar com uma situação de relacionamento. Há uma conexão que não pode ser descrita o mundo é visualizado como mais agradável. Não há incerteza que possa penetrar, nada desconhecido que possa quebrar uma parte, referindo-se a (Energia das Forças Das Trevas). Satanás é ótimo em manter seu povo em relacionamentos incríveis, ambos viajando pelo caminho de Satanás. Satanás também pode ser notado em fazer bons relacionamentos, quando um de seus seguidores está, em um relacionamento com alguém de uma fé diferente. Como dito antes Satanás é antigo, então não há teoria de que Satanás saiba sobre o amor. Não há dúvida de que aqueles no caminho de Satanás terão amor uns com os outros, isto é, claro, se eles querem. Uma relação fundada com a iniciação, é um fogo selvagem abençoado conter ...

Capítulo (5): Poesia sábia de Satanás

Se ao menos você não fosse mal compreendido, quão brilhante será o brilho do céu? Como a formulação da água à vista do meu olho nu leva minha mente aos tempos antigos, você aparece em glória. O mundo é um reflexo de sua existência. Os pensamentos estão cheios de prazeres notáveis. Eu vejo sua beleza, eu quero sua companhia, e eu sei que não deve ser ingênua. Através das nuvens, se eles puderem me segurar de pé sobre eles. Eu vou viajar a distância; Eu vou ancorar ocupando nada, exceto infinito.

1220 (Poesia)

Capítulo (6): Comunidade de Satanás

Ao longo dos tempos, houve comunidades que foram impulsionadas por Satanás. Só porque uma pessoa escolhe seguir o conhecimento proibido e sabedoria de Satanás não faz deles menos do que qualquer outra pessoa compartilhando planeta terra. Uma comunidade de Satanás é uma comunidade que lida com rituais. Eles lidam com a previsão das coisas antes de acontecerem e de estarem bem preparados. Seria uma honra até mesmo ser aceito nas atividades de tal comunidade, enquanto outros podem vê-la diferente. Veja a idade da Terra e as diferentes energias; influências que a maioria das pessoas tomam apenas andando fora ou abrindo uma janela na casa. Ao lidar com a sabedoria e o conhecimento que se pode obter de Satanás, você encontrará muita felicidade, autosatisfação, o que mesmo de uma forma básica é bom porque o aprendizado nunca para. A comunidade de Satanás nunca deve ser descartada porque eles se oferecem para aplicar inteligência onde ela precisa estar. Compreender a inteligência é comum até mesmo para um membro do Caminho de Satanás.

(1220)

Capítulo (7): Como controlar seus pensamentos
Pode Satanás ajudá-lo?

É importante saber que todos temos uma
cabeça cheia de pensamentos e aparecem mais em
tempos de emoções diferentes. Para as pessoas que
vivem do Caminho de Satanás, elas estão
familiarizadas com essa ocorrência diária dentro da
mente. Eles estudaram a si mesmos ao ponto de
poderem escolher seus pensamentos como usar as
mãos, em vez da escolha de ação. Satanás
desempenha um papel importante nessa habilidade
porque é incentivada em algum momento ao se
juntar ao povo satã. Este capítulo está abordando a
consciência de uma área específica do tema, não há
desejo de ser descritivo. Deve-se procurar dominarse em todos os aspectos, especialmente lidar com a
mente. Orientação seria melhor do que tentar
simplesmente entender algo não compreensível.
Satanás quer que seu povo não seja vítima de não ter
autocontrole ou controle de pensamento.

Capítulo (8): A carta do Papa Satânico (Papa-Jaheem R.Hilts)

O Darkside tem sido requintado no desenvolvimento da inteligência, desde sua antiga formulação. A maneira satânica foi discriminada por causa do mal-entendido de Satanás. As pessoas elogiam atos insalubres sobre a humanidade aceitando o erro de certos pares ou parentes e desaprovam a crença religiosa de outra pessoa. Para o futuro do Satânico todos os satânicos devem mostrar a diferença para diminuir a ignorância da percepção da cultura satânica. O futuro do Satânico florescerá em felicidade em todos os seus assuntos. Lembre-se de que estranhos não importam se você está fazendo o certo, mesmo em particular. O crescimento do Satânico será maciço e cuidadosamente aplicado para que as pessoas possam ver a verdade em vez de falso dogma. Não permita que a ignorância ou o julgamento das pessoas façam você questionar a realidade quando ela veio de suas ilusões/ilusão diárias.

Satanic Pope
(1220) *Jaheem R. Hilts*
May 9th, 2020 11:28pm (MST)

Capítulo (9): Resumo sobre o mundo invisível

Era uma vez, em um mundo que só lidava com espíritos, havia uma atividade constante no uso de habilidades sobrenaturais no mundo invisível. Tudo estava acontecendo espíritos estavam dando à luz espíritos; espíritos passaram pelo processo de morrer, mesmo que eles não poderiam morrer. Deus reinou supremo e tudo foi iluminado pelo espírito real, o Criador de todos os existentes. A luz do Trono era a luz do mundo. Satanás era mais experiente do que todos no mundo espiritual. Ele era um mestre e passava um tempo ponderando as coisas existentes. O pensamento passou pela mente de Deus por outra parte de sua criação. Satanás estava cheio de alegria, começou a tocar música que agradou a Deus, os Anjos até cantaram. Então Deus começou a manifestar coisas na existência. Satanás pensou que era uma expansão para o mundo invisível. Satanás viu a glória e a beleza de Deus, ele ficou tentado a falar quando viu Deus formando o homem, então ele esperou........ (Para continuar)

Biblical Scholar
1220-*Jaheem R.Hilts*

Capítulo (10): Satanás deve ser compreendido e não evitado

Se olharmos para toda a história bíblica, a humanidade tomou suas próprias decisões, da sobrevivência à habilidade. Dizem que "Lúcifer foi expulso do céu" eles dizem "Adão e Eva foram expulsos do Jardim do Éden". Não há ninguém para culpar no final do dia. Satanás não deve ser evitado especialmente quando se tem conhecimento de Satanás, mesmo que não o faça. A razão pela qual digo isso é porque todos têm uma escolha de livre arbí8as. De que adiantaria evitar alguém e você tem a escolha de tomar uma decisão que ninguém pode tomar por você. Nós no Satânico abraçamos Satanás porque ele está cheio de sabedoria que o homem não tem capacidade de ter. Temos a menor visão sobre o mundo invisível. Satanás é uma forma diferente de criação; os iniciados podem entender a ampla idade de como se comunicar e entender com o que estão lidando. Satanás deve ser compreendido e não evitado. (1220)

Capítulo (11): A entrada é importante

É importante saber que a entrada no Satânico é sensível, muito delicada. Deve ser um assunto levado muito a sério e não é permitido ser abusado. É um mundo dentro de um mundo, o conhecimento não deve ser desperdiçado. A maioria das pessoas não buscará a verdade e a curiosidade é comum. A importância está além da compreensão dos não iniciados. Aqueles com conhecimento podem querer aumentar o crescimento espiritual; praticar a cultura da unidade satânica. Como se vem para a frente com a capacidade de crescer é importante, o amor pelo Satânico deve ser forte em uma prática de iniciações sobre os outros ou o fracasso é possível. À medida que a luz brilha na escuridão e a escuridão brilha na luz, tudo será. Nunca procure fazer a mente de outra pessoa se render/submissão é para todos os alunos.

Översatt till svenska
Swedish

De mest kunniga vet att har funnits längre än mänskligheten. Missförståndet från den individuella förståelsen av en person eliminerar överseende till högre bekräftelse. Anden kan bara se i mörker, man måste lära sig den förbjudna sanningen att utmärka sig i en resa som är nödvändig i alla ögon, särskilt det tredje ögat. har uppenbarat himmelens och Jordens hemligheter för dem som är mest pålitliga för honom; hans sak att göra ett uttalande. Att tro på hjälp är det delvis att acceptera att även är en del av hela skapelsen. Varför kommer man att se ner på vad de inte förstår? Att hitta på ursäkter för deras handlingar. har en roll i saker som äger rum på Jorden; vissa är njutbara, några som en lektion. Tacka för att du gjorde dig starkare, ge inte upp hoppet om dig själv. (1220)

Kapitel (1): är uråldrig

Från tidernas begynnelse långt innan medvetandet ens var ett alternativ existerade. Universum var bara fullt av andar; andra saker som bara var kapabla i den osynliga världen. Intelligens skulle inte ens förstås på en mänsklig nivå eftersom människor inte existerade, utom i en framtida plan. Aktiviteterna i dessa andliga världar har aldrig kunnat dokumentation. var före kreativitet och strukturell utveckling av arkitektoniska mönster av tidigare generationer av mänskligheten. är gammal eftersom vi inte kan beräkna hans tid i tillvaron, när han föddes eller bildades. Vi skall veta att de i biblisk tid anslöt sig till för visdom och förmågan att se längre än andra. är ingen dåre vi alla har val val var magnifik i hans ögon. Rätt och fel är bara av dem uppfattning, synda har fört lycka till oräkneliga mängder människor dagligen, längre än erkända. behöver inte tänka för dig, du är en del av början, oavsett hur mycket tid som går.

Kapitel (2): Hur man kan hjälpa

Du måste inse att du hjälper att det hjälper dig. vill att du ska ha alla nöjen och önskningar du vill ha för dig själv. Genom att hjälpa kommer du att göra gott för alla synder i världen. Du hjälper genom att hjälpa andra; människor kommer samman och njuta av tid med varandra i sätt, medan synden är vacker, måste du sprida sin skönhet. Att hjälpa bör inte betraktas som en svaghet, även om människor kommer att rynka pannan på verket. Du kan hjälpa genom att inte vara dum föregå med gott exempel, skapa mer fred än de som påstår sig vara gudfruktiga. Du kan hjälpa genom att vara lojal och pålitlig mot armé. Det finns en kamp mellan gott och ont och vill inte bara vara känd för det onda; Förstörelse.

Kapitel (3): Konvertera till

Jag skulle inte råda någon att försöka förstå själva. Det skulle vara större att introduceras till De Mörka krafterna. Man kan förlora hoppet att försöka nå ut till utan att inleda. Förmågan att konvertera är som allt annat, du måste ha tro. Tro på kan inte vara lätt för alla på grund av det negativa skvaller, inspelningar av falska tolkningar. Sinne, kropp och själ måste vara i den för att få fullbordan; ingenting är helt saknas något viktigt. Konvertera till är känslig eftersom det är hemlighetsfull den första processen åtminstone, det är mycket fördelaktigt för dem som är avsedda att konvertera från sina tidigare förvirring. Jag skulle kunna hänvisa till andra böcker för att bredda förståelsen av detta ämne. Jag väljer att inte eftersom de inte kommer att stödja dig konvertera. representerar förbjuden kunskap eller hemlig kunskap. Konvertera till du måste börja utvecklas, efter att ha burit fröna. De kommer att växa även om du motstå dig själv. Konvertera till det är en ny början, en...

Kapitel (4): Relationer &

Sann kärlek är lätt att hitta i två personer som vill vara tillsammans, baserat på förtroende. Det är inte något som gjorts av ett omedvetet beslut båda måste vilja samma sak. Den förbjudna kunskap som förs vidare till initieran är tillräcklig för att hantera en relationssituation. Det finns ett samband som inte kan beskrivas världen visualiseras som trevligare. Det finns ingen osäkerhet som kan tränga in, inget okänt som kan bryta dig en del, med hänvisning till (Dark Forces Energy). är stor i att hålla sitt folk i awesome relationer, båda reser vägen för. kan också noteras för att skapa goda relationer, när en av hans anhängare är, i en relation med någon med en annan tro. Som sagt innan är gammal så det finns ingen teori om att vet om kärlek. Det råder ingen tvekan om att de på väg kommer att älska med varandra, detta är naturligtvis om de vill ha det. En relation som grundades med inledande, är en välsignad vild eld innehålla ...

Kapitel (5): kloka poesi

Om du bara inte missförstods, hur ljust kommer skenet från himlen att vara? Som formulering av vatten i åsynen av mitt blotta ögat leder mitt sinne till antiken, du visas i härlighet. Världen är en återspegling av din existens. Tankarna är fyllda med alldagliga nöjen. Jag ser din skönhet, jag vill ha ditt sällskap, och jag vet att jag inte är naiv. Genom molnen, om de kan hålla mig stående på dem. Jag skall resa avståndet; Jag kommer att förankra ockuperar ingenting annat än oändlig.

1220 (Poesi)

Kapitel (6): Gemenskapen av

Genom tiderna har det funnits samhällen som drevs av. Bara för att en person väljer att följa förbjudna kunskap och visdom gör dem inte mindre än någon annan som delar planeten jorden. En gemenskap av är en gemenskap av är en gemenskap som handlar om ritualer. De handlar om att förutse saker innan de inträffar och vara väl förberedda. Det skulle vara en ära att ens accepteras i verksamheten i ett sådant samhälle, medan andra kan se det annorlunda. Se hur gammal jorden är och de olika energierna; påverkar de flesta människor tar in bara gå utanför eller öppna ett fönster i huset. När man hanterar visdom och kunskap man kan få från, hittar du en hel del lycka, självtillfredsställelse, som även i en grundläggande form är bra eftersom lärandet aldrig slutar. gemenskap bör aldrig kastas eftersom de erbjuder sig att tillämpa intelligens där det behöver vara. Att förstå intelligens är vanligt för ens en medlem av väg.

(1220)

Kapitel (7): Hur man kontrollerar dina tankar kan hjälpa dig?

Det är viktigt att veta att vi alla har ett huvud fullt av tankar och mer visas i tider av olika känslor. För de människor som lever på väg, de är bekanta med denna dagliga händelse i sinnet. De har studerat sig själva till den grad att de kan plocka sina tankar som att använda sina händer, i stället för valet av åtgärder. spelar en viktig roll i denna förmåga eftersom det uppmuntras någon gång när man går med i folk. Detta kapitel berör medvetenheten om ett visst ämnesområde finns det ingen önskan att vara beskrivande. Man måste försöka behärska sig i alla aspekter, särskilt att hantera sinnet. Vägledning skulle vara bättre än att helt enkelt förstå något som inte är förståeligt. vill att hans folk inte ska bli offer för att inte ha självkontroll eller tankekontroll.

Kapitel (8): Brevet från Den sataniska påven (Pope-Jaheem R.Hilts)

Darkside har varit utsökt i utvecklingen av intelligens, sedan dess gamla formulering. Det sataniska sättet har diskriminerats på grund av missförståndet om. Människor berömma hellre ohälsosamma handlingar på mänskligheten acceptera fel från vissa kamrater eller släktingar och rynka pannan på någon annans religiösa tro. För framtiden för Satanic alla sataniska bör visa skillnaden att minska okunnighet om uppfattningen av den sataniska kulturen. Framtiden för det sataniska skall blomstra i lycka i alla dess angelägenheter. Påminn dig själv utomstående spelar ingen roll om du gör rätt, även i privat. Tillväxten av det sataniska skall vara massiv och noggrant tillämpas så att människor kan se sanningen i stället för falska dogmer. Låt inte människors okunnighet eller dom att få dig att ifrågasätta verkligheten när det kom från deras dagliga illusioner / vanföreställningar.

Satanic Pope

(1220) *Jaheem R.Hilts*

May 9th, 2020 11:28pm (MST)

Kapitel (9): Kort om den osynliga världen

En gång i tiden, i en värld som bara handlade om andar, fanns det en ständig aktivitet i att använda övernaturliga förmågor i den osynliga världen. Allt hände andar födde andar; andar gick igenom processen att dö trots att de inte kunde dö. Gud regerade högsta och allt belystes av den kungliga anden, Skaparen av alla som existerar. Ljuset från Tronen var världens ljus. var kunnig mer än alla i den andliga världen. Han var en mästare och han tillbringade tid att begrunda det som finns. Tanken slog Guds sinne för en annan del av hans skapelse. var full av glädje, började han spela musik som gladde Gud, Änglarna sjöng till och med. Då började Gud manifestera saker som existerar. trodde att det var en expansion för den osynliga världen. såg Guds härlighet och skönhet, han var frestad att tala när han såg Gud bilda människa, då väntade han........

(Fortsättning)

Biblical Scholar
1220-*Jaheem R.Hilts*

Kapitel (10): bör förstås och inte skys

Om vi tittar på all biblisk historia mänskligheten har gjort sina egna beslut från överlevnad till förmåga. De säger "Lucifer kastades ut ur himlen" de säger "Adam och Eva kastades från Edens lustgård". Det finns ingen att skylla på i slutet av dagen. bör inte skys särskilt när man har kunskap om, även om man inte gör det. Anledningen till att jag säger detta är att alla har en fri vilja val. Vad bra skulle det vara att undvika någon och du har valet att fatta ett beslut ingen kan göra för dig. Vi i omfamna eftersom han är fylld av visdom som människan inte har någon förmåga att ha. Vi har den minsta insikt om hela den osynliga världen. är en annan form av skapelse; de initierade kan förstå bredden i hur man kommunicerar och förstår vad de har att göra med. bör förstås och inte skys. (1220)

Kapitel (11): Ingången är viktig

Det är viktigt att veta att ingången till Satanic är känslig, mycket känslig. Det bör tas på största allvar och inte tillåtas missbrukas. Det är en värld i en värld, kunskap bör inte slösas bort. De flesta människor kommer inte att söka sanningen och nyfikenhet är vanligt. Betydelsen är obegriplig för den oinvigde. De med kunskap kanske vill ytterligare andlig tillväxt; öva kulturen av Den Satanic enheten. Hur man kommer fram med förmågan att växa är viktigt, kärleken till Satanic måste vara stark i en öva initieringar på andra eller misslyckande är möjligt. När ljuset lyser i mörker och mörker lyser i ljus, kommer allt att vara. Aldrig försöka göra någon annans sinne upp kapitulation / inlämning är för alla elever.

Translated into Thai

Thai

ผู้รอบรู้มากที่สุดจะรู้ว่าซาตานได้อยู่นานกว่ามนุษย์

ความเข้าใจผิดจากความเข้าใจของแต่ละบุคคลจะช่วยลดการปล่อยตัวให้เป็นที่ยอมรับสูง

วิญญาณสามารถเห็นได้ในความมืดเท่านั้นต้องได้รับการสอนความจริงต้องห้ามที่จะเก่งในการเดินทางที่จำเป็นในทุกสายตาโดยเฉพาะตา 3

ซาตานได้เปิดเผยความลับของสวรรค์และโลกให้กับผู้ที่น่าเชื่อถือที่สุดกับเขา เขาจึงกล่าวคำแถลง

การเชื่อในความช่วยเหลือของซาตานก็ยอมรับว่าซาตานเป็นส่วนหนึ่งของการสร้างทั้ง

ทำไมหนึ่งจะมองลงมาสิ่งที่พวกเขาไม่เข้าใจ?

แก้ตัวสำหรับการกระทำของพวกเขา

ซาตานมีบทบาทในสิ่งต่างๆที่เกิดขึ้นบนโลก

บางคนก็สนุก

ขอบคุณซาตานที่ทำให้แกแข็งแกร่งขึ้น (1220)

บทที่ (1): ซาตานเป็นโบราณ

จากจุดเริ่มต้นของเวลานานก่อนสติได้ตัวเลือก, ซาตานมีอยู่.

จักรวาลนั้นเต็มไปด้วยวิญญาณ สิ่งอื่น ๆ ที่มีความสามารถในโลกที่มองไม่เห็นเท่านั้น ปัญญาจะไม่ได้เข้าใจในระดับมนุษย์เพราะมนุษย์ไม่ได้อยู่ยกเว้นในแผนในอนาคต กิจกรรมในอาณาจักรทางจิตวิญญาณเหล่านี้ไม่เคยมีความสามารถในการเอกสาร

ซาตานก่อนความคิดสร้างสรรค์และการพัฒนาโครงสร้างของการออกแบบสถาปัตยกรรมโดยรุ่นที่ผ่านมาของมนุษยชาติ

ซาตานเป็นโบราณเพราะเราไม่สามารถคำนวณเวลาของเขาในการดำรงชีวิตเมื่อเขาเกิดหรือเกิด

เราจะรู้ว่าผู้ที่อยู่ในพระคัมภีร์ไบเบิลครั้งเข้าร่วมซาตานสำหรับภูมิปัญญาและความสามารถในการดูเพิ่มเติมกว่าคนอื่น ๆ

ซาตานไม่โง่เราทุกคนมีทางเลือกของซาตาน

คืองดงามในสายตาของเขาถูกและผิดเป็นเพี
ยงการรับรู้ของคนบาปได้นำความสุขไปนับไม่
ถ้วนของคนทุกวันนานกว่าได้รับการยอมรับ
ซาตานไม่ต้องคิดให้คุณ,
คุณเป็นส่วนหนึ่งของจุดเริ่มต้น,
ไม่ว่าเวลาผ่านไปมากน้อยเพียงใด.

บทที่ (2): วิธีการช่วยซาตาน

คุณต้องตระหนักว่าช่วยซาตาน
ซาตานจะต้องการให้คุณมีความสุขและความ
ปรารถนาที่คุณต้องการสำหรับตัวคุณเอง
โดยการช่วยเหลือซาตานคุณจะทำความดีจา
กความทุกความเสิร์ทในโลก
ท่านช่วยซาตานโดยการช่วยเหลือผู้อื่น
คนมาร่วมกันและสนุกกับเวลากันในแบบซาต
านในขณะที่ความมีความสวยงามคุณต้องกระ
จายความงามของ
การช่วยซาตานไม่ควรได้รับการพิจารณาจุดอ่
อนแม้ว่าคนจะขมขืนเมื่อทำงาน
คุณสามารถช่วยซาตานได้ด้วยการไม่โง่เขลา
นำโดยแบบอย่างสร้างความสงบสุขมากกว่าผู้
ที่เชื่อในพระเจ้า
คุณสามารถช่วยซาตานได้โดยซื่อสัตย์และเชื่
อถือได้ให้กับกองทัพซาตาน
มีการต่อสู้ระหว่างความดีและความอาฆาตแล

263

ะซาตานไม่เพียงต้องการที่จะเป็นที่รู้จักสำหรับความชั่วร้าย ทำลาย

บทที่ (3): การแปลงเป็นซาตาน

ฉันจะไม่แนะนำให้ใครบางคนที่จะพยายามเข้าใจซาตานด้วยตัวเอง
มันจะยิ่งถูกนำเข้าสู่กองกำลังมืด
หนึ่งสามารถสูญเสียความหวังพยายามที่จะติดต่อกับซาตานโดยไม่ต้องเริ่ม
ความสามารถในการเปลี่ยนใจเริศนั้นก็เหมือนสิ่งอื่น
ความเชื่อในซาตานอาจไม่ง่ายสำหรับทุกคนเพราะซุบซิบเชิงลบบันทึกการตีความเท็จ
จิตใจร่างกายและจิตวิญญาณจะต้องอยู่ในนั้นจะได้รับความสมบูรณ์
ไม่มีอะไรที่ขาดหายไปทั้งหมดสิ่งที่สำคัญ
การแปลงเป็นซาตานมีความสำคัญเพราะเป็นความลับ
กระบวนการเริ่มต้นอย่างน้อยก็เป็นประโยชน์อย่างมาก
สำหรับผู้ที่ destined
การแปลงจากความสับสนที่ผ่านมาของพวกเขา
ฉันสามารถอ้างอิงหนังสืออื่น ๆ
เพื่อขยายความเข้าใจของหัวข้อนี้
ฉันเลือกที่จะไม่เพราะพวกเขาจะไม่สนับสนุนคุณแปลง ซาตานหมายถึงความรู้ที่ต้องห้ามหรือความรู้ลับ
แปลงไปซาตานที่คุณต้องเริ่มต้นการพัฒนาหลังจากแบกเมล็ด พวกเขาจะเติบโตแม้ว่าคุณจะต่อต้านตัวเอง
แปลงเป็นซาตานเป็นจุดเริ่มต้นใหม่, ...

บทที่ (4): ความสัมพันธ์ & saa

รักแท้พบได้ง่ายในสองคนที่ต้องการอยู่ด้วยกันขึ้นอยู่กับความไว้วางใจ

มันไม่ได้เป็นอะไรที่ทำให้ปิดการตัดสินใจสติทั้งสองจะต้องต้องการสิ่งเดียวกัน

ความรู้ต้องห้ามที่ส่งต่อไปยังการเริ่มต้นจะเพียงพอในการจัดการสถานการณ์ความสัมพันธ์

มีการเชื่อมต่อที่อธิบายไม่ได้ว่าโลกเป็นภาพเป็นที่น่ารื่นรมย์มากขึ้นคือ

มีความไม่แน่นอนที่สามารถเจาะไม่ไม่มีอะไรที่ไม่รู้จักที่สามารถทำลายคุณเป็นส่วนหนึ่งหมายถึง

(พลังเข้มพลังงาน)

ซาตานเป็นที่ดีในการรักษาคนของเขาในความสัมพันธ์ที่น่ากลัวทั้งสองเดินทางเส้นทางของซาตาน

ซาตานยังสามารถได้รับการกล่าวถึงในการสร้างความสัมพันธ์ที่ดีเมื่อผู้ติดตามคนหนึ่งของเขาคือในความสัมพันธ์กับคนที่มีความเชื่อต่างกัน

ตามที่ระบุไว้ก่อนที่ซาตานเป็นโบราณจึงมีทฤษฎีที่ซาตานรู้เกี่ยวกับความรักไม่มี

มีคำถามว่าผู้ที่อยู่บนเส้นทางซาตานจะมีความรักซึ่งกันและกันนี้แน่นอนคือถ้าพวกเขาต้องการมัน

ความสัมพันธ์ที่ก่อตั้งขึ้นกับ initiation

เป็นป่าบรรจุไฟจำเริ...

266

บท (5): บทกวีปรีชาญาณของซาตาน

ถ้าเพียงคุณเข้าใจผิด,
จะเรืองแสงจากท้องฟ้าจะสดใสแค่ไหน?
เมื่อการคิดค้นน้ำในสายตาของตาเปล่าของฉันทำให้จิ
ตใจของฉันเป็นสมัยโบราณคุณปรากฏในพระสิริ
โลกเป็นภาพสะท้อนของการดำรงอยู่ของคุณ
ความคิดที่เต็มไปด้วยความสุขที่ไม่ธรรมดา
ฉันเห็นความงามของคุณ
ผ่านเมฆถ้าพวกเขาสามารถถือฉันยืนอยู่บนพวกเขา
ฉันจะเดินทางไกล ฉันจะยึดครองอะไรยกเว้นอนันต์

1220 (บทกวี)

บทที่ (6): ชุมชนของซาตาน

ตลอดวัยมีชุมชนที่ถูกขับเคลื่อนโดยซาตาน เพียงเพราะคนเลือกที่จะทำตามความรู้ต้องห้ามและภูมิปัญญาของซาตานไม่ได้ทำให้พวกเขาน้อยกว่าคนอื่นแบ่งปันโลกดาวเคราะห์

ชุมชนของซาตานเป็นชุมชนที่เกี่ยวข้องกับพิธีกรรม พวกเขาจัดการกับสิ่งที่มองเห็นก่อนที่พวกเขาเกิดขึ้นและถูกเตรียมดี

มันจะเป็นเกียรติที่ได้ยอมรับในกิจกรรมของชุมชนดังกล่าวในขณะที่คนอื่นอาจเห็นมันแตกต่างกัน

ดูซิว่าแผ่นดินโลกเก่าและพลังงานที่แตกต่างกัน อิทธิพลที่คนส่วนใหญ่ใช้เวลาเพียงเดินนอกหรือเปิดหน้าต่างในบ้าน

เมื่อจัดการกับภูมิปัญญาและความรู้หนึ่งจะได้รับจากซาตาน, คุณจะพบมากความสุข,

ความพึงพอใจในตนเองซึ่งแม้ในรูปแบบพื้นฐานเป็นสิ่งที่ดีเพราะการเรียนรู้ไม่เคยหยุด.

ชุมชนของซาตานไม่ควรละทิ้งเพราะพวกเขาเสนอที่จะใช้ปัญญาที่จะต้องมีการ

การเข้าใจสติปัญญาเป็นเรื่องธรรมดาสำหรับแม้แต่สมาชิกคนหนึ่งของเส้นทางซาตาน (1220)

บทที่ (7):
วิธีควบคุมความคิดของคุณซาตานสามารถช่วยให้คุณ
?

มันเป็นสิ่งสำคัญที่จะรู้ว่าเราทุกคนมีหัวเต็มของความคิดและปรากฏในช่วงเวลาของอารมณ์ที่แตกต่างกัน
สำหรับคนที่อาศัยอยู่นอกเส้นทางซาตานพวกเขาจะคุ้นเคยกับเหตุการณ์ประจำวันนี้ภายในใจ
พวกเขาได้ศึกษาตัวเองไปยังจุดที่พวกเขาสามารถเลือกความคิดของพวกเขาเช่นการใช้มือของพวกเขาแทนการเลือกของการกระทำ
ซาตานมีบทบาทสำคัญในความสามารถนี้เพราะได้รับการสนับสนุนในบางจุดเมื่อเข้าร่วม The Satan คน.
บทนี้สัมผัสในการรับรู้ของพื้นที่เฉพาะของหัวข้อที่มีความปรารถนาที่จะบรรยายไม่เป็น
หนึ่งต้องพยายามที่จะโทตัวเองในทุกด้านโดยเฉพาะอย่างยิ่งการจัดการกับจิตใจ
คำแนะนำจะดีกว่าการพยายามที่จะเข้าใจสิ่งที่ไม่เข้าใจ
ซาตานต้องการให้คนของเขาไม่ตกเป็นเหยื่อของการไม่มีการควบคุมตนเองหรือการควบคุมความคิด

บทที่ (8):
จดหมายจากสมเด็จพระสันตะปาปาซาตาน
(สมเด็จพระสันตะปาปาเจี้ยม R.Hilts)

Darkside
ได้ประณีตในการพัฒนาปัญญาตั้งแต่สูตรโบราณ
วิธีซาตานได้รับการเลือกปฏิบัติในเพราะความเข้าใจผิ
ดของซาตาน
คนค่อนข้างสรรเสริญการกระทำที่ไม่แข็งแรงกับมนุษ
ย์ยอมรับผิดจากเพื่อนหรือญาติบางและขมขต่อความเ
ชื่อทางศาสนาของคนอื่น
สำหรับอนาคตของซาตานซาตานทั้งหมดควรแสดงคว
ามแตกต่างเพื่อลดความไม่รู้ของการรับรู้ของวัฒนธรร
มซาตาน
อนาคตของซาตานจะเจริญรุ่งเรืองในความสุขในทุกกิ
จการของตน
เตือนตัวเองว่าบุคคลภายนอกไม่สำคัญว่าคุณกำลังทำ
ถูกต้องแม้ในภาคเอกชน
การเจริญเติบโตของซาตานจะใหญ่และใช้อย่างระมัด
ระวังเพื่อให้ประชาชนสามารถมองเห็นความจริงแทนก
ารผิด
ไม่อนุญาตให้ผู้คนไม่รู้หรือตัดสินที่จะทำให้คุณถามคว

270

ามเป็นจริงเมื่อมันมาจากภาพลวงตาประจำวัน /
ความเข้าใจผิดของพวกเขา

Satanic Pope
(1220) *Jaheem R.Hilts*
May 9th, 2020 11:28pm (MST)

บทที่ (9): บทสรุปเกี่ยวกับโลกที่มองไม่เห็น

กาลครั้งหนึ่งในโลกเท่านั้นที่จัดการกับสุรามีกิ
จกรรมอย่างต่อเนื่องในการใช้ความสามารถเหนือธรรม
ชาติในโลกที่มองไม่เห็น
ทุกอย่างเกิดขึ้นวิญญาณได้เกิดกับวิญญาณ
วิญญาณผ่านกระบวนการตายแม้ว่าพวกเขาจะตาย
พระเจ้าทรงครองอำนาจสูงสุดและทุกอย่างถูกส่องสว่
างโดยพระวิญญาณพระผู้สร้างของทั้งหมดในการดำร
งอยู่ แสงจากบัลลังก์เป็นแสงสว่างของโลก
ซาตานมีความรู้มากกว่าทั้งหมดในโลกทางวิญญาณ
เขาเป็นนายและเขาใช้เวลาไตร่ตรองสิ่งต่าง ๆ
ในการดำรงอยู่
ความคิดข้ามใจของพระเจ้าสำหรับส่วนหนึ่งของการส
ร้างของเขาอีก
ซาตานเต็มไปด้วยความสุขเขาเริ่มเล่นเพลงที่พระเจ้า
พระเจ้าแม้ร้องเพลง
แล้วอัลลอฮฺได้ทรงเริ่มการเผยให้เห็นบางสิ่ง
ที่มีอยู่ในนั้น
ซาตานคิดว่ามันเป็นการขยายตัวของโลกที่มองไม่เห็น
ซาตานเห็นพระสิริของพระเจ้าและความงามเขาถูกล่อ
ลวงให้พูดเมื่อเขาเห็นพระเจ้าหล่อมนุษย์แล้วเขารอ
(จะต่อ)

Biblical Scholar
1220-*Jaheem R.Hilts*

บทที่ (10): ซาตานควรเข้าใจและไม่ถูกรังเกียจ

ถ้าเราดูทุกประวัติศาสตร์ในพระคัมภีร์มนุษย์ได้ตัดสินใจของเขาจากความอยู่รอดเพื่อความสามารถ
พวกเขากล่าวว่า "ลูซิเฟอร์ถูกขับออกจากสวรรค์"
พวกเขากล่าวว่า
"อาดัมและเอวาถูกขับออกจากสวนเอเดน"
ไม่มีใครที่จะตำหนิณ สิ้นวัน
ซาตานไม่ควรถูกรังเกียจโดยเฉพาะอย่างยิ่งเมื่อหนึ่งมีความรู้ของซาตานแม้ว่าหนึ่งไม่ได้
เหตุผลที่ผมพูดนี้เป็นเพราะทุกคนมีทางเลือกอิสระ
สิ่งที่ดีจะ shun
ใครสักคนและคุณมีตัวเลือกในการตัดสินใจไม่มีใครสามารถทำให้สำหรับคุณ
เราอยู่ในซาตานโอบกอดซาตานเพราะเขาเต็มไปด้วยภูมิปัญญาที่มนุษย์มีความสามารถในการมีไม่ได้
เรามีความเข้าใจที่น้อยที่สุดในโลกที่มองไม่เห็นเต็ม
ซาตานเป็นอีกรูปแบบหนึ่งของการสร้าง;
ผู้ริเริ่มสามารถเข้าใจกว้างของวิธีการสื่อสารและเข้าใจสิ่งที่พวกเขากำลังติดต่อกับ
ซาตานควรจะเข้าใจและไม่ถูกรังเกียจ (1220)

บทที่ (11): ทางเข้าเป็นสิ่งสำคัญ

สิ่งสำคัญคือต้องรู้ว่าทางเข้าเข้าสู่ซาตานมีความละเอียดอ่อนละเอียดอ่อนมาก

มันควรจะเป็นเรื่องที่ถ่ายอย่างจริงจังและไม่ได้รับอนุญาตให้ถูกทำร้าย

มันเป็นโลกในโลกที่ความรู้ไม่ควรสูญเปล่า

คนส่วนใหญ่จะไม่แสวงหาความจริงและความอยากรู้อยากเห็นเป็นเรื่องธรรมดา

ความสำคัญนั้นเกินความเข้าใจของมือใหม่

ผู้ที่มีความรู้อาจต้องการการเติบโตทางวิญญาณเพิ่มเติม ปฏิบัติวัฒนธรรมของความสามัคคีซาตาน

วิธีหนึ่งมาข้างหน้ามีความสามารถในการเติบโตเป็นสิ่งสำคัญ,

ความรักสำหรับซาตานจะต้องแข็งแกร่งในการฝึกฝนหนึ่งในผู้อื่นหรือความล้มเหลวเป็นไปได้.

เมื่อแสงส่องในความมืดและความมืดส่องในแสงก็จะเป็น ไม่พยายามทำให้คนอื่นใจขึ้นยอมจำนน /

ส่งสำหรับนักเรียนทุกคน.

Перевод на русский язык
Russian

Самые знающие будут знать, что сатана был вокруг дольше, чем человечество. Непонимание индивидуального понимания человека устраняет снисхождение к высшему признанию. Дух может видеть только во тьме, нужно учить запретной истине преуспеть в путешествии, необходимом во всех глазах, особенно в третьем глазу. Сатана открыл тайны Неба и Земли тем, кто больше всего заслуживает доверия к нему; его причина, чтобы сделать заявление. Верить в помощь сатаны, это частично смирилось с тем, что даже сатана является частью всего творения. Почему смотреть сничто вниз на то, что они не понимают? Оправдываться за свои действия. Сатана играет определенную роль в вещах, происходящих на Земле; некоторые из них приятными, некоторые в качестве урока. Спасибо сатане за то,

что сделали тебя сильнее, не сдавайтесь.
(1220)

Глава (1): Сатана древний

С самого начала времени задолго до того, сознание было даже вариант, сатана существовал. Вселенная была просто полна духов; другие вещи, которые были способны только в невидимом мире. Интеллект даже не будет понят на человеческом уровне, потому что людей не существует, за исключением будущего плана. Деятельность в этих духовных сферах никогда не была способна к документированию. Сатана был до творчества и структурного развития архитектурных конструкций прошлых поколений человечества. Сатана стар, потому что мы не можем рассчитать его время в существовании, когда он родился или сформировался. Мы будем знать тех, кто в библейские времена присоединился к сатане, для мудрости и способности видеть дальше, чем другие. Сатана не дурак у всех нас есть выбор, выбор сатаны был великолепным в его глазах. Право и неправильно только те восприятие, грешный принес счастье бесчисленное количество людей ежедневно, дольше, чем признается. Сатана не должен думать за вас, вы являетесь частью начала, независимо от того, сколько времени проходит.

Глава (2): Как помочь сатане

Ты должен понять, что ты помогаешь сатане, что это помогает тебе. Сатана захочет, чтобы у вас были все удовольствия и желания, которые вы хотите для себя. Помогая сатане, вы сделаете добро на все грехи в мире. Вы помогаете сатане, помогая другим; люди собираются вместе и наслаждаться временем друг с другом в сатане пути, в то время как грех прекрасен, вы должны распространять свою красоту. Помощь сатане не должна рассматриваться как слабость, даже если люди будут хмуриться на работе. Вы можете помочь сатане, не будучи глупым, ведя пример, создавая больше мира, чем те, кто исповедует, чтобы быть Божественным. Вы можете помочь сатане, будучи лояльным и надежным к армии Сатаны. Существует битва между добром и злом, и сатана не просто хочет быть известным злом; Уничтожения.

Глава (3): Преобразование в сатану

Я бы не советовал кому-то пытаться понять сатану самостоятельно. Было бы больше, чтобы быть введены в Темные силы. Можно потерять надежду, пытаясь протянуть руку помощи сатане без посвящения. Способность обратиться, как и все остальное, вы должны иметь веру. Вера в сатану может быть нелегкой для всех из-за негативных сплетен, записей ложных интерпретаций. Разум, тело и душа должны быть в нем, чтобы получить завершение; ничто не является целым отсутствует что-то важное. Преобразование в сатану является чувствительным, потому что это скрытный первоначальный процесс, по крайней мере, это очень полезно для тех, кому суждено преобразовать из своих прошлых путаницы. Я мог бы ссылаться на другие книги, чтобы расширить понимание этой темы. Я выбираю не делать этого, потому что они не будут поддерживать вас преобразования. Сатана представляет собой запрещенное знание или тайное знание. Преобразование в сатану вы должны начать развиваться, после проведения семян. Они будут расти, даже если вы сопротивляетесь себе. Преобразование в сатану это новое начало, ...

Глава (4): Отношения и сатана

Истинная любовь легко найти в двух людей, желающих быть вместе, на основе доверия. Это не что-нибудь сделал от бессознательного решения как придется хотеть то же самое. Запрещенное знание, которое передается инициаку, достаточно для урегулирования ситуации отношений. Существует связь, которую нельзя описать, мир визуализируется как более приятный. Существует нет неопределенности, которая может проникнуть, ничего неизвестного, что может сломать вам часть, ссылаясь на (Темные силы энергии). Сатана велик в сохранении своего народа в удивительных отношений, как путешествие по пути сатаны. Сатана также может быть отмечен в создании хороших отношений, когда один из его последователей, в отношениях с кем-то другой веры. Как было сказано, прежде чем сатана является древним, так что нет теории, что сатана знает о любви. Существует никаких сомнений в том, что те, на пути сатаны будут иметь любовь друг с другом, это, конечно, если они хотят его. Отношения

основаны с посвящением, является благословил
дикий огонь содержать ...

Глава (5): Мудрая поэзия сатаны

Если бы вас не поняли, насколько ярким будет свечение с неба? Как формулировка воды в глазах моего невооруженным глазом приводит мой взгляд, в древние времена, вы появляются в славе. Мир является отражением вашего существования. Мысли наполнены ничем не примечательными удовольствиями. Я вижу твою красоту, я хочу, чтобы ваша компания, и я знаю, не быть наивным. Сквозь облака, если они могут держать меня стоя на них. Я пройду расстояние; Я буду якорь, занимая ничего, кроме бесконечного.

1220 (Поэзия)

Глава (6): Сообщество Сатаны

На протяжении веков были общины, которые были обусловлены сатаной. Просто потому, что человек выбирает следовать запрещенным знаниям и мудрости сатаны не делает их меньше, чем кто-либо другой обмена планеты Земля. Община сатаны – это сообщество, которое занимается ритуалами. Они имеют дело с предвидя вещи, прежде чем они происходят и быть хорошо подготовлены. Было бы честью даже быть принятым в деятельность такого сообщества, в то время как другие могут видеть его по-другому. Посмотрите, сколько лет земле и различные энергии; влияет большинство людей принять в просто ходить на улицу или открытие окна в доме. При работе с мудростью и знаниями можно получить от сатаны, вы найдете много счастья, самоудовлетворения, которые даже в основной форме хорошо, потому что обучение никогда не останавливается. Община сатаны никогда не должна быть отброшена, потому что они предлагают применять интеллект там, где он должен быть. Понимание интеллекта

является общим даже для одного члена Пути
Сатаны.
   (1220)

Глава (7): Как контролировать свои мысли может сатана помочь вам?

Важно знать, что у всех нас есть голова, полная мыслей и более появляются во времена различных эмоций. Для людей, которые живут за счет Пути Сатаны, они знакомы с этим повседневным явлением в уме. Они изучили себя до такой степени, что они могут выбрать свои мысли, как с помощью своих рук, а не выбор действий. Сатана играет важную роль в этой способности, потому что это поощряется в какой-то момент при присоединении к народу сатаны. В этой главе затрагивается осознание конкретной области темы нет никакого желания быть описательным. Нужно стремиться овладеть собой во всех аспектах, особенно в отношении ума. Руководство было бы лучше, чем пытаться просто понять что-то непонятное. Сатана хочет, чтобы его народ не был жертвой отсутствия самоконтроля или контроля над мыслями.

Глава (8): Письмо Сатанинского Папы (Папа-Джахим Р. Хилтс)

Darkside был изысканным в развитии интеллекта, так как его древняя формулировка. Сатанинский путь был дискриминирован из-за непонимания сатаны. Люди скорее хвалят нездоровые поступки в отношении человечества, принимая неладное от некоторых сверстников или родственников, и хмурятся на чужие религиозные убеждения. Для будущего сатанинского все сатанинские должны показать разницу, чтобы уменьшить незнание восприятия сатанинской культуры. Будущее Сатанинской должен процветать в счастье во всех своих делах. Напомните себе аутсайдеров не имеет значения, если вы делаете правильно, даже в частном порядке. Рост сатанинской должны быть массовыми и тщательно применяться, чтобы люди могли видеть правду, а не ложные догмы. Не позволяйте народам невежества или суждения, чтобы заставить вас вопрос реальности, когда он пришел из своих ежедневных иллюзий / обмана.

Satanic Pope
(1220) *Jaheem R. Hilts*
May 9th, 2020 11:28pm (MST)

Глава (9): Краткое описание невидимого мира

Давным-давно, в мире, имеющем дело только с духами, была постоянная активность в использовании сверхъестественных способностей в невидимом мире. Все, что происходило духи рождали духов; духи прошли через процесс смерти, даже если они не могли умереть. Бог царствовал, и все было освещено царским духом, Творцом всего существования. Свет от Трона был светом мира. Сатана был хорошо осведомлен больше, чем все в духовном мире. Он был мастером, и он провел время размышлял вещи в существовании. Мысль пересекла разум Бога для другой части его творения. Сатана был полон радости, он начал играть музыку, которая радовала Бога, Ангелы даже пели. Тогда Бог начал проявлять вещи в существовании. Сатана думал, что это расширение для невидимого мира. Сатана видел Славу И красоту Бога, он был соблазн говорить, когда он увидел Бога формирования человека, то он ждал … …..

(Чтобы быть продолжена)

Biblical Scholar
1220-*Jaheem R.Hilts*

Глава (10): Сатану следует понимать, а не избегать

Если мы посмотрим на всю библейскую историю человечество приняло свои собственные решения от выживания до способности. Они говорят: "Люцифер был изгнан с небес" они говорят: "Адам и Ева были отлиты из Эдемского сада". Существует не кого винить в конце дня. Сатану не следует избегать, особенно когда человек знает о сатане, даже если он этого не делает. Причина, по которой я говорю это, в том, что у каждого есть выбор свободной воли. Что хорошего было бы избегать кого-то, и у вас есть выбор, чтобы принять решение никто не может сделать для вас. Мы в Сатанинском объятии сатаны, потому что он наполнен мудростью, которую человек не имеет. У нас есть малейшее представление о полном невидимом мире. Сатана – это другая форма творения; инициированные могут понять широту того, как общаться и понять, с чем они имеют дело. Сатану следует понимать, а не избегать. (1220)

Глава (11): Вход важен

Важно знать, что вход в Сатанинскую чувствительна, очень деликатна. Это вопрос должен быть очень серьезно и не допустить злоупотребления. Это мир внутри мира, знания не должны быть потрачены впустую. Большинство людей не будут искать истину и любопытство является общим. Важность непомерно поймяется. Те, у кого есть знания, могут захотеть дальнейшего духовного роста; практиковать культуру сатанинского единства. Как один приходит вперед с способностью расти важно, любовь к сатанинской должны быть сильными в одном практикующих посвящений на других или неудачи возможно. Как свет светит в темноте и тьма светит в свете, все это будет. Никогда не стремитесь сделать чужой ум до капитуляции / представления для всех студентов.

Tradus în limba română
Romanian

Cei mai bine cunoscătoare vor ști că Satana a fost în preajma omenirii. Neînțelegerea de la înțelegerea individuală a unei persoane elimină indulgența în recunoaștere mai mare. Spiritul poate vedea doar în întuneric, trebuie să fie învățat adevărul interzis să exceleze într-o călătorie necesară în toți ochii, în special al treilea ochi. Diavolul a dezvăluit tainele Cerului și ale Pământului celor mai de încredere pentru el. cauza lui de a face o declarație. Pentru a crede în ajutorul lui Satana, este parțial acceptarea că, chiar Satana este o parte a întregii creații. De ce se va uita în jos la ceea ce ei nu înțeleg? Inventând scuze pentru acțiunile lor. Satana are un rol în lucrurile care au loc pe Pământ; unele sunt plăcute, altele ca o lecție. Mulțumește-i lui Satan pentru că te-a făcut mai puternic, nu renunța la tine. (1220)

Capitolul (1): Satana este antic

De la începutul timpului, cu mult înainte ca conștiința să fie o opțiune, Satana a existat. Universul era plin de spirite; alte lucruri care au fost capabile doar în lumea nevăzută. Inteligența nici măcar nu ar fi înțeleasă la nivel uman pentru că oamenii nu existau, decât într-un plan viitor. Activitățile din aceste tărâmuri spirituale nu au fost niciodată capabile de documentare. Satana a fost înainte de creativitatea și dezvoltarea structurală a desenelor arhitecturale de către generațiile trecute ale omenirii. Satana este străvechi pentru că nu-i putem calcula timpul existent, când s-a născut sau s-a format. Îi vom cunoaște pe cei din timpurile biblice care s-au alăturat lui Satan pentru înțelepciune și capacitatea de a vedea mai departe decât alții. Satana nu este un prost noi toți avem alegeri alegerea lui Satana a fost magnific în ochii lui. Binele și răul sunt doar prin percepția celor, păcatul a adus fericire a nenumărate cantități de oameni de zi cu zi, mai mult decât a recunoscut. Satana nu trebuie să se gândească pentru tine, ești o parte a începutului, indiferent de cât de mult timp trece.

Capitolul (2): de a ajuta Satana

Trebuie să-ți dai seama că-l ajuți pe Satana, te ajută. Satana va dori să aveți toate plăcerile și dorințele pe care le doriți pentru voi înșivă. Ajutându-l pe Satana, vei face bine tuturor păcatelor din lume. Îl ajutați pe Satana ajutându-i pe alții; oamenii se unesc și se bucură de timp unii cu alții în moduri satanice, în timp ce păcatul este frumos, trebuie să-i împrăștii frumusețea. A-l ajuta pe Satana nu trebuie considerat o slăbiciune, chiar dacă oamenii se vor încrunta în lucrare. Îl puteți ajuta pe Satana prin a nu fi prost, conducând prin exemplu, creând mai multă pace decât cei care pretind că sunt evlavioși. Îl poți ajuta pe Satana fiind loial și de încredere în Armata Satanei. Există o bătălie între bine și rău și Satana nu vrea doar să fie cunoscut pentru rău; Distrugere.

Capitolul (3): Convertirea la Satana

Nu aș sfătui pe cineva să încerce să-l înțeleagă pe Satana de la sine. Ar fi mai mult să fie introdus în The Dark Forces. Se poate pierde speranța încercarea de a ajunge la Satana fără inițiere. Abilitatea de a converti este ca orice altceva, trebuie să ai credință. Credința în Satana s-ar putea să nu fie ușoară pentru toată lumea din cauza bârfelor negative, a înregistrărilor unor interpretări false. Mintea, trupul și sufletul trebuie să fie în ea pentru a primi finalizarea; Nimic nu lipsește ceva important. Convertirea la Satana este sensibilă pentru că este secretoasă procesul inițial, cel puțin, este extrem de benefic pentru cei destinați să se convertească din confuziile lor din trecut. Aș putea face referire la alte cărți pentru a lărgi înțelegerea acestui subiect. Aleg să nu o fac pentru că nu te vor sprijini să te convertești. Satana reprezintă cunoașterea interzisă sau cunoașterea secretă. Convertindu-vă la Satana, trebuie să începeți să vă dezvoltați, după ce cărați semințele. Vor crește chiar dacă te opui. Convertirea la Satana este un nou început, un ...

Capitolul (4): Relații & Satana

Dragostea adevărată este ușor de găsit în două persoane care doresc să fie împreună, pe baza încrederii. Nu e nimic luat de pe o decizie inconștientă ambele vor trebui să vrea același lucru. Cunoașterea interzisă care este transmisă inițiatorului este suficientă în gestionarea unei relații. Există o conexiune care nu poate fi descrisă că lumea este vizualizată ca fiind mai plăcută. Nu există nici o incertitudine care poate pătrunde, nimic necunoscut care vă poate rupe o parte, referindu-se la (Dark Forces Energy). Satana este mare în păstrarea poporului său în relații minunat, ambele călătoresc calea lui Satana. Satana poate fi, de asemenea, remarcat în a face relații bune, atunci când unul dintre adepții săi este, într-o relație cu cineva de o credință diferită. După s-a spus înainte, Satana este străveche, deci nu există nici o teorie că Satana știe despre dragoste. Nu există nici o îndoială că cei de pe calea Satana va avea dragoste unul cu altul, acest lucru este, desigur, dacă doresc. O relație fondată cu inițierea, este un foc sălbatic binecuvântat conține ...

Capitolul (5): Poezia înțeleaptă a lui Satan

Dacă nu ai fi înțeles greșit, cât de strălucitoare va fi strălucirea din cer? Ca formularea de apă în vederea cu ochii mei cu ochii înșiprui conduce mintea mea la cele mai vechi timpuri, apar în glorie. Lumea este o reflectare a existenței tale. Gândurile sunt pline de plăceri neremarcabile. Îți văd frumusețea, vreau compania ta, și știu că nu vreau să fiu naivă. Printre nori, dacă mă pot ține stând pe ei. Voi călători de la distanță; Voi ancora ocupând nimic în afară de infinit.

1220 (Poezie)

Capitolul (6): Comunitatea satanei

De-a lungul veacurilor au existat comunități care au fost conduse de Satana. Doar pentru că o persoană alege să urmeze cunoașterea interzisă și înțelepciunea lui Satana nu le face mai puțin decât oricine altcineva de partajare planeta pământ. O comunitate a satanei este o comunitate care se ocupă de ritualuri. Ei se ocupă cu prevăzând lucruri înainte ca acestea să se întâmple și să fie bine pregătiți. Ar fi o onoare să fie chiar acceptate în activitățile unei astfel de comunități, în timp ce alții pot vedea diferit. Uite cât de vechi este pământul și energiile diferite; influențează cei mai mulți oameni să ia în doar de mers pe jos în afara sau deschiderea unei ferestre în casă. Când ai de-a face cu înțelepciunea și cunoașterea se poate obține de la Satana, veți găsi o mulțime de fericire, satisfacție de sine, care chiar și într-o formă de bază este bun, deoarece învățarea nu se oprește niciodată. Comunitatea lui Satana nu trebuie niciodată aruncată pentru că se oferă să aplice inteligența acolo unde trebuie. Înțelegerea inteligenței este comună chiar și pentru un membru al Căii Satanei. (1220)

Capitolul (7): să vă controlați gândurile vă poate ajuta Satana?

Este important să știm că toți avem un cap plin de gânduri și mai apar în momente de emoții diferite. Pentru oamenii care trăiesc de pe Calea Satanei, ei sunt familiarizați cu această apariție de zi cu zi în interiorul minții. Ei s-au studiat până la punctul în care pot alege gândurile lor ca folosind mâinile lor, în loc de alegerea de acțiune. Satana joacă un rol major în această abilitate, deoarece este încurajat la un moment dat atunci când se alătură poporului Satan. Acest capitol este atingerea cu privire la conștientizarea unui anumit domeniu de subiect nu există nici o dorință de a fi descriptiv. Trebuie să căutăm să ne stăpânim în toate aspectele, în special în ceea ce privește mintea. Orientarear fi mai bine decât încercarea de a înțelege pur și simplu ceva nu este de înțeles. Satana vrea ca poporul său să nu fie victime ale faptului că nu au control sau gândire.

Capitolul (8): Scrisoarea Papei Satanic (Papa-Jaheem R.Hilts)

Darkside a fost rafinat în dezvoltarea de inteligenta, de la formularea sa veche. Calea satanică a fost discriminată din cauza neînțelegerii lui Satan. Oamenii laudă mai degrabă acte nesănătoase asupra umanității acceptarea greșit de la anumite colegii sau rude și încruntare a credinței altcuiva religioase. Pentru viitorul satanic toate satanic ar trebui să arate diferența de a reduce ignoranța de percepție a culturii satanice. Viitorul Satanic va înflori în fericire în toate afacerile sale. Amintește-ți că străinii nu contează dacă faci bine, chiar și în particular. Creșterea satanic va fi masivă și aplicată cu atenție, astfel încât oamenii să poată vedea adevărul în loc de dogmă falsă. Nu permite popoarelor ignoranță sau hotărâre pentru a vă face să întrebare realitate atunci când a venit de la iluziile lor de zi cu zi / iluzie.

Satanic Pope

(1220) *Jaheem R.Hilts*

May 9th, 2020 11:28pm (MST)

Capitolul (9): Scurt despre lumea nevăzută

A fost odată ca niciodată, într-o lume care se ocupă doar de spirite, a existat o activitate constantă în utilizarea abilităților supranaturale în lumea nevăzută. Totul se întâmpla spiritele dădeau naștere spiritelor; Spiritele au trecut prin procesul de a muri, chiar dacă nu puteau muri. Dumnezeu a domnit suprem și totul a fost luminat de spiritul regal, Creatorul tuturor celor existenți. Lumina de pe Tron a fost lumina lumii. Satana a fost cunoscătoare mai mult decât toate în lumea spirituală. El a fost un maestru și a petrecut timp cugetând lucrurile existente. Gândul a trecut prin mintea lui Dumnezeu pentru o altă parte a creației Sale. Satana era plin de bucurie, a început să cânte muzică care l-a mulțumit pe Dumnezeu, Îngerii chiar cântau. Apoi, Dumnezeu a început să manifeste lucruri în existență. Satana a crezut că este o expansiune pentru lumea nevăzută. Satana a văzut slava și frumusețea lui Dumnezeu, el a fost ispitit să vorbească când l-a văzut pe Dumnezeu formând omul, apoi a așteptat...

(A se continua)

Biblical Scholar
1220-*Jaheem R.Hilts*

Capitolul (10): Satana trebuie înțeleasă și nu evitată

Dacă ne uităm la toată istoria biblică, omenirea a luat propriile decizii de la supraviețuire la abilitate. Se spune că "Lucifer a fost alungat din Cer" se spune că "Adam și Eva au fost aruncați din Grădina Edenului". Nu e nimeni de vină la sfârșitul zilei. Satana nu ar trebui să fie evitate mai ales atunci când unul are cunoștințe de Satana, chiar dacă unul nu. Motivul pentru care spun acest lucru este pentru că toată lumea are o alegere libera. La ce bun să te ferești de cineva și ai posibilitatea de a lua o decizie pe care nimeni nu o poate lua pentru tine. Noi, cei din Satana, îl îmbrățișăm pe Satana pentru că el este plin de înțelepciune pe care omul nu are capacitatea de a o avea. Avem cea mai mică perspectivă asupra lumii nevăzute. Satana este o formă diferită de creație; cei inițiați pot înțelege cât de larg ă a modului de a comunica și de a înțelege cu ce se confruntă. Satana trebuie înțeles și nu evitat. (1220)

Capitolul (11): Intrarea este importantă

Este important de știut că intrarea în Satanic este sensibilă, foarte delicată. Ar trebui să fie o chestiune luată foarte în serios și să nu fie permisă să fie abuzată. Este o lume în interiorul unei lumi, cunoașterea nu trebuie irosită. Cei mai mulți oameni nu vor căuta adevărul și curiozitatea este comună. Importanța este dincolo de înțelegerea celor neinițiați. Cei cu cunoștințe pot dori să continue creșterea spirituală; practica cultura unității satanice. Modul în care cineva vine înainte cu capacitatea de a crește este important, dragostea pentru Satanic trebuie să fie puternic într-o practicarea initieri pe alții sau eșecul este posibil. Pe măsură ce lumina strălucește în întuneric și întunericul strălucește în lumină, totul va fi. Nu încercați să faceți mintea altcuiva până predare / depunerea este pentru toți studenții.

Traducido al español
Spanish

Los más informados sabrán que Satanás ha existido más tiempo que la humanidad. El malentendido de la comprensión individual de una persona elimina la indulgencia en un mayor reconocimiento. El espíritu sólo puede ver en la oscuridad, uno debe ser enseñado la verdad prohibida para sobresalir en un viaje necesario en todos los ojos, especialmente el tercer ojo. Satanás ha revelado secretos del Cielo y la Tierra a los más confiables para él; su causa para hacer una declaración. Creer en la ayuda de Satanás, es parcialmente aceptar que incluso Satanás es parte de toda la creación. ¿Por qué uno mira hacia abajo en lo que no entiende? Poniendo excusas para sus acciones. Satanás tiene un papel en las cosas que tienen lugar en la Tierra; algunos son agradables, otros como una lección. Da gracias a Satanás por hacerte más fuerte, no te rindas. (1220)

Capítulo (1): Satanás es antiguo

Desde el principio de los tiempos mucho antes de que la conciencia fuera una opción, Satanás existió. El universo estaba lleno de espíritus; otras cosas que sólo eran capaces en el mundo no visto. La inteligencia ni siquiera se entendería a nivel humano porque los humanos no existían, excepto en un plan futuro. Las actividades en estos reinos espirituales nunca han sido capaces de documentación. Satanás estaba ante la creatividad y el desarrollo estructural de los diseños arquitectónicos por generaciones pasadas de la humanidad. Satanás es antiguo porque no podemos calcular su tiempo en la existencia, cuando nació o se formó. Conoceremos a aquellos en tiempos bíblicos que se unieron a Satanás por sabiduría y la capacidad de ver más lejos que otros.

Satanás no es tonto, todos tenemos opciones que la elección de Satanás fue magnífica a sus ojos. El bien y el mal son simplemente por la percepción de los unos, el pecado ha llevado la felicidad a innumerables cantidades de personas diariamente, más largas de lo que se reconoce. Satanás no tiene que pensar por ti, eres parte del principio, no importa cuánto tiempo pase.

Capítulo (2): Cómo ayudar a Satanás

Tienes que darte cuenta de que ayudas a Satanás te está ayudando. Satanás querrá que tengas todos los placeres y deseos que deseas para ti mismo. Al ayudar a Satanás, harás bien todos los pecados del mundo. Ayudas a Satanás ayudando a los demás; la gente se une y disfruta del tiempo el uno con el otro de maneras satanásas, mientras que el pecado es hermoso, debes difundir su belleza. Ayudar a Satanás no debe considerarse una debilidad, a pesar de que la gente frunce el ceño sobre la obra. Puedes ayudar a Satanás al no ser tonto dirigiendo con el ejemplo, creando más paz que aquellos que profesan ser piadosos. Puedes ayudar a Satanás siendo leal y confiable para el Ejército de Satanás. Hay una batalla entre el bien y el mal y Satanás

no sólo quiere ser conocido por el mal;
Destrucción.

Capítulo (3): Convertirse a Satanás

No aconsejaría a alguien que trate de entender a Satanás por sí mismo. Sería mayor ser introducido a las Fuerzas Oscuras. Uno puede perder la esperanza tratando de tender la mano a Satanás sin iniciación. La capacidad de convertirse es como todo lo demás, tienes que tener fe. La fe en Satanás puede no ser fácil para todos debido a los chismes negativos, las grabaciones de interpretaciones falsas. La mente, el cuerpo y el alma tienen que estar en ella para recibir la finalización; nada falta algo importante. Convertirse a Satanás es sensible porque es secreto el proceso inicial al menos, es altamente beneficioso para aquellos destinados a convertirse de sus confusiones pasadas. Podría hacer referencia a otros libros para ampliar la comprensión de este tema. Elijo no hacerlo porque no te apoyarán convirtiendo. Satanás representa el conocimiento prohibido o el conocimiento secreto. Al convertirte a Satanás tienes que comenzar a desarrollarte, después de llevar las semillas. Crecerán incluso si te resistes a ti mismo. Convertir a Satanás es un nuevo comienzo, un ...

Capítulo (4): Relaciones & Satanás

El amor verdadero se encuentra fácilmente en dos personas que quieren estar juntas, basadas en la confianza. No es nada hecho una decisión inconsciente que ambos tendrán que querer lo mismo. El conocimiento prohibido que se transmite al iniciado es suficiente para manejar una situación de relación. Hay una conexión que no se puede describir el mundo se visualiza como más agradable. No hay incertidumbre que pueda penetrar, nada desconocido que pueda romperte una parte, refiriéndose a (Energía de Fuerzas Oscuras). Satanás es grande al mantener a su pueblo en relaciones increíbles, ambos viajando por el camino de Satanás. Satanás también se puede notar al hacer buenas relaciones, cuando uno de sus seguidores lo es, en una relación con alguien de una fe diferente. Como se dijo antes de que Satanás sea antiguo, no hay teoría que Satanás sepa sobre el amor. No hay duda de que aquellos en el camino de Satanás tendrán amor el uno con el otro, esto es por supuesto si lo quieren. Una relación fundada con la iniciación, es un bendito fuego salvaje que contiene ...

Capítulo (5): Poesía sabia de Satanás

Si no te hubieran malinterpretado, ¿cuán brillante será el resplandor del cielo? Como la formulación del agua a la vista de mi ojo desnudo lleva mi mente a los tiempos antiguos, apareces en gloria. El mundo es un reflejo.de tu existencia. Los pensamientos están llenos de placeres poco notables. Veo tu belleza, quiero tu compañía, y sé que no debeser ingenua. A través de las nubes, si pueden mantenerme de pie sobre ellas. Voy a viajar la distancia; Anclaré ocupando nada excepto infinito.

1220 (Poesía)

Capítulo (6): Comunidad de Satanás

A través de los siglos ha habido comunidades que fueron impulsadas por Satanás. El hecho de que una persona decida seguir el conocimiento y la sabiduría prohibidos de Satanás no los hace menos que nadie que comparta el planeta tierra. Una comunidad de Satanás es una comunidad que se ocupa de los rituales. Se ocupan de prever las cosas antes de que sucedan y estar bien preparados. Sería un honor incluso ser aceptado en las actividades de tal comunidad, mientras que otros pueden verlo diferente. Mira la edad de la tierra y las diferentes energías; influye en que la mayoría de las personas tienen en caminar afuera o abrir una ventana en la casa. Al tratar con la sabiduría y el conocimiento que uno puede obtener de Satanás, encontrará una gran cantidad de felicidad, auto satisfacción, que incluso en una forma básica es buena porque el aprendizaje nunca se detiene. La comunidad de Satanás nunca debe ser descartada porque ofrecen aplicar inteligencia donde tiene que estar. Comprender la inteligencia es común incluso para un miembro de The Satan Path. (1220)

Capítulo (7): ¿Cómo controlar sus pensamientos puede ayudarle Satanás?

Es importante saber que todos tenemos la cabeza llena de pensamientos y más aparecen en tiempos de diferentes emociones. Para las personas que viven de El Sendero Satanás, están familiarizadas con esta ocurrencia diaria dentro de la mente. Se han estudiado hasta el punto de que pueden elegir sus pensamientos como usar sus manos, en lugar de la elección de la acción. Satanás desempeña un papel importante en esta habilidad porque se alienta en algún momento al unirse al pueblo Satanás. Este capítulo está tocando la conciencia de un área específica del tema que no hay deseo de ser descriptivo. Uno debe tratar de dominarse a sí mismo en todos los aspectos, especialmente tratando con la mente. La orientación sería mejor que tratar de simplemente entender algo que no es comprensible. Satanás quiere que su pueblo no sea víctima de no tener autocontrol o control de pensamiento.

Capítulo (8): La carta del Papa Satánico (Papa-Jaheem R.Hilts)

El Darkside ha sido exquisito en el desarrollo de la inteligencia, desde su antigua formulación. La manera satánica ha sido discriminada debido al malentendido de Satanás. La gente más bien elogia los actos insalubres sobre la humanidad aceptando el mal de ciertos compañeros o parientes y frunciendo el ceño sobre la creencia religiosa de otra persona. Para el futuro de El Satánico todo satánico debe mostrar la diferencia para disminuir la ignorancia de la percepción de la cultura satánica. El futuro de Los satánicos florecerá en felicidad en todos sus asuntos. Recuérdate que los forasteros no importan si estás haciendo lo correcto, incluso en privado. El crecimiento de The Satanic será masivo y cuidadosamente aplicado para que la gente pueda ver la verdad en lugar de un dogma falso. No permitas que la ignorancia o el juicio de los pueblos te hagan cuestionar la realidad cuando proviene de sus ilusiones/delirios diarios.

Satanic Pope
(1220) *Jaheem R.Hilts*
May 9th, 2020 11:28pm (MST)

Capítulo (9): Breve sobre el mundo no visto

Había una vez, en un mundo que sólo se ocupaba de los espíritus, había una actividad constante en el uso de habilidades sobrenaturales en el mundo invisible. Todo lo que sucedía, los espíritus daban a luz a los espíritus; los espíritus pasaron por el proceso de morir a pesar de que no podían morir. Dios reinó supremo y todo fue iluminado por el espíritu real, el Creador de todos en existencia. La luz del Trono era la luz del mundo. Satanás era más conocedor que todos en el mundo espiritual. Era un maestro y pasaba tiempo meditando en las cosas que existían. El pensamiento cruzó la mente de Dios por otra parte de su creación. Satanás estaba lleno de gozo, comenzó a tocar música que complacía a Dios, los ángeles incluso cantaron. Entonces Dios comenzó a manifestar las cosas en la existencia. Satanás pensó que era una expansión para el mundo no visto. Satanás vio la gloria y la belleza de Dios, se sintió tentado a hablar cuando vio a Dios formando al hombre, entonces esperó........

(Continuar)

Biblical Scholar
1220-*Jaheem R.Hilts*

Capítulo (10): Satanás debe ser comprendido y no rechazado

Si miramos toda la historia bíblica, la humanidad ha tomado sus propias decisiones desde la supervivencia hasta la habilidad. Dicen que "Lucifer fue expulsado del cielo" dicen "Adán y Eva fueron expulsados de El Jardín del Edén". No hay nadie a quien culpar al final del día. Satanás no debe ser rechazado especialmente cuando uno tiene conocimiento de Satanás, incluso si uno no lo hace. La razón por la que digo esto es porque todo el mundo tiene una opción de libre albedita. De qué sería bueno rechazar a alguien y tienes la opción de tomar una decisión que nadie puede tomar por ti. Nosotros en El Satánico abrazamos a Satanás porque está lleno de sabiduría que el hombre no tiene capacidad de tener. Tenemos la más mínima visión sobre el mundo inédita. Satanás es una forma diferente de creación; los iniciados pueden entender la amplitud de cómo comunicarse y entender con qué están tratando. Satanás debe ser comprendido y no rechazado. (1220)

Capítulo (11): La entrada es importante

Es importante saber que la entrada en El Satánico es sensible, muy delicada. Debe ser un asunto tomado muy en serio y no se le permite ser abusado. Es un mundo dentro de un mundo, el conocimiento no debe ser desperdiciado. La mayoría de la gente no buscará la verdad y la curiosidad es común. La importancia está más allá de la comprensión de los no iniciados. Aquellos con conocimiento tal vez deseen un mayor crecimiento espiritual; practicar la cultura de La unidad satánica. La forma en que uno presenta la capacidad de crecer es importante, el amor por El Satánico debe ser fuerte en una practicando iniciaciones en los demás o el fracaso es posible. A medida que la luz brille en la oscuridad y la oscuridad brille en la luz, todo será. Nunca trate de hacer que la mente de otra persona se rinda / la sumisión es para todos los estudiantes.

한국어 번역

Korean

가장 잘 아는 사람은 사탄이 인류보다 더 오래 주변에 있었다는 것을 알게 될 것입니다. 개인의 이해에서 오해는 더 높은 인정에 탐닉을 제거합니다. 영은 어둠 속에서만 볼 수 있으며, 모든 눈, 특히 제 3 의 눈에 필요한 여행에서 뛰어나기 위해 금지 된 진리를 가르쳐야합니다. 사탄은 자신에게 가장 신뢰할 만한 사람들에게 하늘과 땅의 비밀을 밝혔습니다. 진술을 할 수 있습니다. 사탄의 도움을 믿기 위해, 사탄조차도 전체 창조의 일부라는 것을 부분적으로 받아들이고 있습니다. 왜 그들은 이해하지 못하는 것을 내려다 볼 것인가? 그들의 행동에 대한 변명. 사탄은 지상에서 일어나는 일에서 중요한 역할을 합니다. 일부는 즐거운, 일부는 교훈으로. 여러분을 더

강하게 만들어 주신 사탄에게 감사를
드리고, 자신을 포기하지 마십시오.
(1220)

장 (1): 사탄은 고대인

의식이 선택사항이되기 훨씬 전부터 사탄은 존재했습니다. 우주는 단지 영으로 가득 차 있었다. 보이지 않는 세상에서만 할 수 있었던 다른 것들. 미래의 계획을 제외하고는 인간이 존재하지 않았기 때문에 지능은 인간 수준에서도 이해되지 않을 것입니다. 이 영적 영역에서의 활동은 결코 문서화할 수 없었습니다. 사탄은 과거 세대의 인류가 건축 디자인의 창의성과 구조적 발전을 하기 전에 있었다. 사탄은 우리가 태어나거나 형성되었을 때, 존재할 때 그의 시간을 계산할 수 없기 때문에 고대입니다. 우리는 성경 시대에 사탄이 지혜와 다른 사람들보다 더 멀리 볼 수 있는 능력을 위해 사탄에

합류했다는 것을 알게 될 것입니다. 사탄은 우리 모두가 사탄의 선택이 그의 눈에 훌륭했다 선택의 바보가 아니다. 옳고 그수는 단지 사람의 인식에 의한 것이며, 죄는 매일 수많은 사람들에게 행복을 가져다 주었으며, 인식보다 더 길었습니다. 사탄은 당신을 위해 생각할 필요가 없습니다, 당신은 시작의 일부입니다, 아무리 많은 시간이 지나간다.

제2장: 사탄을 돕는 방법

여러분은 사탄이 여러분을 돕고 있다는 것을 깨달아야 합니다. 사탄은 당신이 원하는 모든 즐거움과 욕망을 갖기를 원할 것입니다. 사탄을 도움으로써 여러분은 세상의 모든 죄를 선을 이룰 것입니다. 여러분은 다른 사람들을 도우며 사탄을 돕습니다. 사람들은 함께 모여 사탄의 방법으로 서로 시간을 즐길 수, 죄는 아름다운 동안, 당신은 그 아름다움을 확산해야합니다. 사람들이 그 사업에 눈살을 찌푸리더라도 사탄을 돕는 것은 약점으로 간주되어서는 안 됩니다. 여러분은 사탄이 모범으로 인도하는 어리석은 인도를 받지 않고, 경건하다고 공언하는 것보다 더 많은 평안을 창조함으로써 사탄을 도울 수

있습니다. 여러분은 사탄군대에
충성하고 신뢰할 수 있게 함으로써
사탄을 도울 수 있습니다. 선과 악
사이에는 싸움이 있으며 사탄은
악으로만 알려지길 원하지 않습니다.
파괴.

장 (3): 사탄으로 개종

저는 누군가에게 사탄을 스스로
이해하라고 권고하지 는 않을 것입니다.
어둠의 세력에 소개되는 것이 더 좋을
것입니다. 개시없이 사탄에게 다가가려는
희망을 잃을 수 있습니다. 개종할 수 있는
능력은 다른 모든 것과 마찬가지로 신앙을
가져야 합니다. 사탄을 믿는 신앙은 부정적인
험담, 거짓 해석의 기록 때문에 모든 사람에게
쉽지 않을 수도 있습니다. 마음과 몸과 영혼이
완성을 받으려면 그 안에 있어야 합니다.
중요한 것을 완전히 놓친 것은 없습니다.
사탄으로 개종하는 것은 적어도 초기 과정이
비밀스러이기 때문에 민감하며, 과거의
혼란에서 개종할 운명을 가진 사람들에게는
매우 유익합니다. 나는 이 주제에 대한 이해를
넓히기 위해 다른 책을 참조 할 수 있었다.
나는 그들이 당신이 변환을 지원하지 않기
때문에 하지 않기로 선택합니다. 사탄은
금지된 지식이나 비밀 지식을 나타냅니다.
사탄으로 개종하면 씨앗을 들고 나서 발전을

시작해야 합니다. 당신이 자신을
저항하더라도 그들은 성장할 것입니다.
사탄으로 개종하는 것은 새로운 시작입니다.

장 (4): 관계와 사탄

진정한 사랑은 신뢰를 바탕으로 함께하고 싶어하는 두 사람에서 쉽게 찾을 수 있습니다. 그것은 둘 다 같은 것을 원할 것입니다 무의식적인 결정을 내린 아무것도 아니다. 수습생에게 전달되는 금지된 지식은 관계 상황을 처리하는 데 충분합니다. 세상이 더 쾌적하게 시각화되어 있다고 설명할 수 없는 연결이 있습니다. 관통할 수 있는 불확실성은 없으며, (암흑세력 에너지)을 언급하여 부품을 깨뜨릴 수 있는 것은 알 수 없습니다. 사탄은 사탄의 길을 여행하는 멋진 관계에서 그의 백성들을 유지하는 데 훌륭합니다. 사탄은 또한 그의 추종자 중 한 명이 다른 신앙을 가진 사람과의 관계에서 좋은 관계를 맺는 데 주목할 수 있습니다. 사탄이 고대에 앞서 언급했듯이, 사탄이 사랑에 대해 알고 있다는 이론은 없습니다. 사탄의 길에 있는 사람들이 서로 사랑을 가질 것이라는 데는 의심의 여지가 없으며, 이것은 물론 그들이 원한다면 입니다. 개시와 함께

설립 된 관계는 축복 된 산불이 포함되어
있습니다 ...

장 (5): 사탄의 현명한 시

당신이 오해하지 않았다면, 하늘에서 빛이 얼마나 밝을 것인가? 내 육안으로 물의 배합이 내 마음을 고대로 이끌때, 당신은 영광에 나타난다. 세상은 당신의 존재를 반영합니다. 생각은 놀라운 즐거움으로 가득차 있습니다. 나는 당신의 아름다움을 보고, 나는 당신의 회사를 원하고, 나는 순진하지 알고있다. 구름을 통해, 그들이 나를 붙잡을 수 있다면 그들 위에 서 있다. 나는 거리를 여행 할 것이다; 나는 무한을 제외하고 는 아무것도 차지하지 앵커 것입니다.

1220 (시)

제6장: 사탄 공동체

오랜 세월 동안 사탄이 이끄는 공동체가 있었습니다. 사람이 사탄의 금지된 지식과 지혜를 따르기로 선택한다고 해서 지구를 공유하는 다른 누구보다도 적게 만들지는 않습니다. 사탄의 공동체는 의식을 다루는 공동체입니다. 그들은 일이 일어나기 전에 일을 예견하고 잘 준비되는 것을 다룹니다. 그러한 공동체의 활동에 받아들여지는 것은 영광일 것이고, 다른 사람들은 그것을 다르게 볼 수도 있습니다. 지구가 얼마나 오래되었고 다른 에너지를 보라. 대부분의 사람들이 그냥 밖으로 산책 하거나 집에서 창을 여는에 걸릴 영향. 사탄에게서 얻을 수 있는 지혜와 지식을 다룰 때, 여러분은 기본적인 형태로도 학습이 멈추지 않을 것이기 때문에 많은 행복과 자기 만족을 발견하게 될 것입니다. 사탄 의 공동체는 필요한 곳에 지능을 적용하겠다고 제안하기 때문에 결코 버려서는 안 됩니다.

사탄의 길에서 한 명이라도 지능을 이해한다.
(1220)

장 (7): 사탄이 여러분을 도울 수 있는 생각을 어떻게 통제하는가?

우리 모두는 생각으로 가득 찬 머리를 가지고 있으며 다른 감정의 시대에 더 많이 나타난다는 것을 아는 것이 중요합니다. 사탄의 길에서 벗어난 사람들에게 그들은 마음 속에서 매일 일어나는 일들을 잘 알고 있습니다. 그들은 행동의 선택 대신 손을 사용하는 것과 같은 생각을 선택할 수 있는 지점까지 스스로를 연구했습니다. 사탄은 사탄 백성들과 함께 할 때 어느 시점에서 격려되기 때문에 이 능력에서 중요한 역할을 합니다. 이 장에서는 설명하려는 욕구가 없는 주제의 특정 영역에 대한 인식을 다지고 있습니다. 사람은 특히 마음을 다루는 모든 면에서 자신을 마스터하기 위해 노력해야합니다. 지침은 단순히 이해할 수없는 무언가를 이해하려고노력하는 것보다 더 좋을 것입니다. 사탄은 백성들이 자제력을

갖지 못하거나 생각을 통제하지 못하는
희생자가 되기를 원합니다.

장 (8): 사탄 교황의 편지 (교황 자헴 R.힐츠)

다크사이드는 고대 의제부터 지능의 발달에 절묘하게 자리잡고 있습니다. 사탄의 방식은 사탄에 대한 오해 때문에 차별을 받았습니다. 사람들은 오히려 특정 동료 나 친척에서 잘못을 받아들이고 다른 사람의 종교적 믿음에 눈살을 찌푸리게 하는 인류에 대한 건강에 해로운 행위를 칭찬합니다. 사탄의 미래를 위하여 모든 사탄은 사탄 문화에 대한 인식의 무지를 줄이는 차이를 보여야 한다. 사탄의 미래는 모든 사무에서 행복으로 번성할 것입니다. 외부인이 사적인 일이라도 옳은 일을 하고 있는지는 중요하지 않다는 것을 상기시켜 주세요. 사탄의 성장은 사람들이 거짓 교리가 아닌 진리를 볼 수 있도록 거대하고 신중하게 적용되어야 한다. 사람들이 무지하거나 판단하는 것이 일상적인 환상/망상에서 비롯될 때 현실에 의문을 품도록 허용하지 마십시오.

Satanic Pope
(1220) *Jaheem R.Hilts*
May 9th, 2020 11:28pm (MST)

장 (9): 보이지 않는 세계에 대한 간략한 설명

옛날 옛적에, 단지 영을 다루는 세계에서, 보이지 않는 세계에서 초자연적인 능력을 사용하는 지속적인 활동이 있었다. 모든 일이 일어나고 있는 영은 영을 낳고 있었다. 영혼은 죽을 수 없었지만 죽어가는 과정을 거쳤습니다. 하나님은 최고를 다스리시고 모든 것이 왕의 영, 즉 모든 존재의 창조주께서 비추신 것입니다. 왕좌의 빛은 세상의 빛이었습니다. 사탄은 영적인 세상에서 그 어느 누구보다도 지식이 풍부했습니다. 그는 주인이었고, 그는 존재하는 것들을 깊이 생각하면서 시간을 보냈다. 그 생각은 하나님의 창조물의 또 다른 부분을 위해 하나님의 마음을 가로질렀다. 사탄은 기쁨으로 가득차 있었고, 그는 하나님을 기쁘게 하는 음악을 연주하기 시작했고, 천사들은 노래를 부르기까지 했다. 그런 다음 하나님은 현존하는 것들을

나타내기 시작하셨습니다. 사탄은 그것이
보이지 않는 세상을 위한 확장이라고
생각했습니다. 사탄은 하나님의 영광과
아름다움을 보았고, 하나님이 사람을
형성하는 것을 보았을 때 말하고 싶은 유혹을
받았고, 그 때 기다렸다.......
　(계속)

Biblical Scholar
1220-*Jaheem R. Hilts*

장 (10): 사탄은 이해되어야 하며 피하지 말아야 한다.

우리가 모든 성경의 역사를 보면 인류는 생존에서 능력에 자신의 결정을 내렸다. 그들은 "루시퍼가 천국에서 쫓겨났다"고 말하며 "아담과 이브는 에덴 동산에서 쫓겨났다"고 말합니다. 하루의 끝에 비난 할 사람이 없다. 사탄은 사탄에 대한 지식이 있을 때, 그렇지 않더라도 특히 피해서는 안 됩니다. 내가 이것을 말하는 이유는 모두가 자유 의지 선택을 하기 때문입니다. 누군가를 피하는 것이 얼마나 좋은 일입니까 그리고 당신은 아무도 당신을 위해 할 수없는 결정을 내릴 수있는 선택의 여지가 있습니다. 사탄에 있는 우리는 사탄을 품에 안아 주는데, 왜냐하면 사탄은 사람이 가질 능력이 없다는 지혜로 가득 차 있기 때문입니다. 우리는 보이지 않는 세상에 대한 사소한 통찰력을 가지고 있습니다. 사탄은 다른 형태의 창조물입니다. 시작된 사람들은 의사 소통하는 방법의 광범위함을 이해하고 그들이 다루는 것을 이해할 수 있습니다.
사탄은 이해되어야 하며 피하지 말아야
합니다. (1220)

장 (11): 입구가 중요합니다.

사탄의 입구는 민감하고 매우 섬세하다는 것을 아는 것이 중요합니다. 그것은 매우 심각하게 촬영하고 학대 수 없습니다 문제이어야 한다. 그것은 세계 내부의 세계이며, 지식을 낭비해서는 안됩니다. 대부분의 사람들은 진실을 추구하지 않으며 호기심은 일반적입니다. 그 중요성은 미숙한 사람들을 이해할 수 없습니다. 지식이 있는 사람들은 영적인 성장을 더 하기를 원할 수도 있습니다. 사탄의 단합문화를 실천한다. 어떻게 성장할 수 있는 능력이 앞으로 나아오는가가 하는 것이 중요하며, 사탄에 대한 사랑은 다른 사람에 대한 개시를 실천하는 데 강해야 하며, 실패가 가능할 수도 있습니다. 어둠 속에서 빛이 비추고 어둠이 빛으로 비출 때, 그것은 모두 될 것입니다. 다른 사람의 마음을 포기/제출하는 것은 모든 학생을 위한 것입니다.